There's No Toilet Paper...

on the
Road Less Traveled

TRAVELERS' TALES GUIDES

There's No Toilet Paper...

on the Road Less Traveled

THE BEST
of Travel Humor and Misadventure

Collected and Edited by

DOUG LANSKY

TRAVELERS' TALES, INC.

SAN FRANCISCO, CALIFORNIA

Humor is not a trick.

Humor is a presence in the world—

like grace—

and shines on everybody.

—GARRISON KEILLOR

Table of Contents

Introduction

Misadventure struck me most recently in—of all places—the men's room of a public library in Holland.

What happened was...when I entered the men's room, I was confronted by not one, but three toilet stalls that I could not open. And unlike most stalls in the U.S., there was nothing to crawl under or climb over. Each stall was its own tiny room. There were small slots in the doors about where the handles should have been, and I thought perhaps the slots were for some kind of coin-operated door system. So I pushed every Dutch coin in my pocket into the hole—even a few German ones. No luck.

Finally, I went out to seek the help of the rotund library security guard. "Of course you can't get into the toilet," he told me in a booming voice that echoed across the crowded study area. "There's no handle."

About fifty heads turned towards me. I wanted to yell out and assure them, "I'm not just a dopey foreigner who couldn't find his way into the toilet," but I realized that's exactly what I was.

"Where does one get a toilet handle?" I asked. He pointed me towards the circulation desk. I slapped my forehead. "The circulation desk. Of course!"

I headed back to the bathroom with renewed confidence. I inserted the handle into one of the doors (one that wasn't jammed with German coins), opened it, stepped inside, and the door swung shut behind me. It was pitch black. And I couldn't find the light. I found something that felt like a light switch, but it didn't do anything except make a clicking sound. I groped around a little more, but I didn't want to grope too much for fear of finding Paleolithic wads of chewed gum and fossilized boogers. I reached over to open the door, but it was locked. After feeling with my hands, I realized I needed the handle to open it. And I had left the handle in the door...on the outside!

I banged on the door. "Help," I said with as friendly and unalarmed a voice as I could muster. A moment later I was rescued by a passing urinator.

Not surprisingly, the humor of this little misadventure didn't really occur to me until I told the story to some friends the next day and they laughed at my flush—I mean brush—with the security guard.

While misadventures may be the most memorable parts of a trip, they are generally embarrassing and frustrating—and rarely seem to be very funny while they are occurring. I've found, while traveling the world non-stop for the last six years gathering adventures (and misadventures) for "Vagabond," my syndicated newspaper column, that the most popular pieces have been the ones describing trips when the most things went wrong, thus proving to me that what makes for a good vacation does not necessarily make for good reading.

The object of this book was to put together a collection of stories by travelers who share a knack for finding the humor in their misadventures and pointing out the absurdities of travel. What absurdities of travel? Perhaps travel writer Bill Bryson sums this up best: "You fly off to a strange land, eagerly abandoning all the comforts of home, and then ex-pend vast quantities of time and money in a largely futile attempt to recapture the comforts that you wouldn't have lost if you hadn't left home in the first place."

And there seems to be no shortage of absurdities these days now that travel is the world's largest industry, raking in $3 trillion annually while taking 500 million people worldwide from X to Y and back to X. Especially since it is largely propelled by vacations that "pamper," offer exotic refrigerator-magnet souvenirs, and give tourists a chance to meet interesting foreigners, sometimes even from different tour groups.

In compiling the stories for this book, it didn't take long to realize the vast range of people's senses of humor. What made a few people laugh until they were foaming at the mouth didn't make another even blow a single spit bubble. What made a man laugh didn't get a rise out of a woman, what made one generation laugh fell flat at the feet of another…you get the picture. It also seems one can get a false sense of unified national humor from watching TV sitcoms which use laugh tracks to let you know when you're supposed to crack up. Like yawning, it's often contagious. If you took away all the dubbed hysterics and had people watch the same sitcoms alone, the differences in senses of humor would become more pronounced. Such is the case when reading humor. In short, if there's a story you don't find particularly funny, rest assured that our careful, mind-numbing research found that several people nearly wet themselves while reading it.

But the biggest challenge of this book was finding a suitable title. The publishers and I kicked around several we hoped would capture the literary essence of this project, such as: *I Ran Over Arthur Frommer on the Road Less Traveled*, *Imodium for the Soul*, and *Off the Beaten Path Through the Back*

Door On a Shoestring for $5 a Day! but we eventually decided on...well, you know what it's called. You may have bought the book on impulse, but the chances are you managed to read the large, bold-faced title at some point before you got it to the cash register, unless you are standing and reading this in the bookstore, in which case I feel obligated to point out that you are loitering.

—Doug Lansky

ALAN ZWEIBEL

* * *

Nudity is a State of Mind

*The author discovers that being naked
is not a spectator sport.*

LET ME JUST SAY AT THE OUTSET THAT AS I WRITE THESE words, I am fully clothed. Shirt. Pants. Shoes. You know the look. Now, this is a point writers rarely feel the need to make. Traditionally, they simply go about the task of setting down words with little or no mention as to which parts of their anatomy are covered or exposed. I envy those writers. I used to be one of them. Allow me to explain.

About a month ago, the pressures of script deadlines made the task of arranging dialogue between characters running around on a movie screen an all-consuming one—to the extent that any distraction was deemed so intrusive, I was absolutely livid when pulled out of a rehearsal to take a call.

"Alan, would you ever give any thought to spending time at a nudist club and writing it up?"

"Yes."

"You can go there whenever you…"

"Yes."

"And you can write the piece whenever you…"

"Yes."

"Any idea when you might be able…"

"Now."

"I mean, you're extremely busy, so…"

"Now."

"But all of your other projects…"

"They can wait. How much do I owe you?"

"For…?"

"Letting me do this."

A CALL TO MY WIFE:

"Hello?"

"Hey, Robin! Guess what? I've been asked to write about a nudist club in Palm Springs."

"I'm not going."

"Who invited you?"

Reaction from the rest of my family ranged from my son, Adam, 14, begging me to take him along, to my youngest daughter, Sari, 7, who giggled at the thought of "Daddy seeing lots of tushies," to my embarrassed middle daughter, Lindsay, 11, who—as I left in the third inning of her West L.A. softball game—found it easier to tell her teammates I was going to the hospital for minor back surgery.

There were other reactions as well. The most asked question: Are you going to get naked? The least asked: Well, my dad lost sleep over where I was going to insert my room key when playing naked volleyball. The person with the most questions: Me. And I started asking them as I turned onto I-10 heading east toward the desert: Why am I doing this? Did I bring enough sunblock? Why am I doing this? When was the last time I was naked in front of a nude woman whom I wasn't married to and with whom I shared a hamper and three children? What if I run into someone I know? Like Siskel? Or Ebert? Or one of my mother's friends? What if I get an erection? What if I get an erection in front of one of my mother's friends? Why am I doing this? And why in God's name am I sweating this much?

The air-conditioning in the car was on full blast, yet as I got closer and closer to the exit that would lead me to the land of naked people, my pores were involuntarily soaking every stitch of fabric associated with my 44-year-old body, and I was now sort of hoping that somewhere between my daughter's softball field and all of those windmill things, I'd contracted malaria and would have to call my editor with my regrets and suggest she send a non-Jewish male to research this article.

The place I was driving toward? The Terra Cotta Inn, which, according to the brochure, was a "clothing optional" resort. So with the distinct possibility that it was nerves and not a rare tropical disease that was causing me to sweat like a fountain, I began to hang onto the word *optional* the way that actress in *Cliffhanger* hung onto Sylvester Stallone's hand.

I can't remember ever knocking more gently than I did on the big gray doors that separate the Terra Cotta Inn from the traffic on East Racquet Club Road. But after a few seconds, the door opened. A woman, dressed only in a romper unzipped to her navel, greeted me. Standing beside her was a completely naked man.

"Alan?"

"Yes."

"I'm Mary Clare."

"Hello."

"And this is my husband, Tom."

"Hi, Alan."

"Nice to meet your penis, Tom."

Rendered mute by their unique brand of desert hospitality, I obediently followed Mary Clare and Tom around a half wall, which gave way to a courtyard. With a pool. Bordered on three sides by attached rooms. And swimming in the pool, lying on the grass near the pool, reading books and Sunday papers on lounge chairs that surrounded the pool and walking around, casually sipping drinks nowhere near the pool, were them—the naked people. Two-eyed, four-cheeked naked people, who obviously didn't know the meaning of the word "optional."

My hosts couldn't have been nicer. They explained that this was strictly a couples resort, where people come with their significant unclothed others to enjoy the sun and relax. The last thing they want is for anyone to feel pressured into walking around in any way that would make them uncomfortable.

——— ☽ ———

While visiting Papua, New Guinea a few years ago, I stopped in a curio shop and impulsively bought a penis gourd, the sole item of attire for the well-dressed Aboriginal male. I thought it would make a splendid addition to the collection of primitive artifacts in my New York apartment.

I picked one from several on display. The saleswoman took my money and, without so much as a flicker of a smile, said, "Shall I wrap it, sir, or will you be wearing it?"

Indeed.

◆

—Ron Butler, "Bad Memories," *Travel & Leisure*

But as much as I appreciated the inherent logic of this policy, anyone who has ever been the only sober person at a party knows how it's possible to feel like the only one who's drunk under those circumstances. I, for one, had never felt goofier than when I was unloading the car.

The fact that I brought luggage to a nudist resort is, in itself, worthy of some discussion. But how I felt carrying three suitcases and a hanging garment bag through a maze of lounging naked people on the way to my room on the far side of the pool is a topic Talmudic rabbis could debate for centuries. Suffice it to say that Robin did my packing, and it took me close to 45 minutes to determine what I was actually going to wear to a naked tea. My decision? Gym shorts and a Yankees nightshirt that extended just below the knee. My thinking? Hard to say. But for some reason, it felt just right.

The office of the Terra Cotta Inn is not dissimilar to the office of any typical resort that happens to have 36 stark-naked adults and one large Jewish man in a Yankees nightshirt having wine and hors d'oeuvres on a Sunday afternoon. Husbands. And wives. Girlfriends. And boyfriends. Youngish. And oldish. Blackish. And whitish. Chitchatting about the weather. The Dodgers. Clinton. Conspicuous by its absence was any overt acknowledgment of each other's overabundance of exposed flesh. They were all so natural. And casual.

Could I possibly be like that? So cool? So nonchalant? I went outside to where everyone had drifted back to their previous locations in and around the pool. I took off my gym shorts. No big deal—courtesy of my Yankees nightshirt—but a start. And then? Oh, what the hell. Off came the nightshirt, and into the pool I dove. Butt naked. Like the day I was born, only larger and more immature.

Under the water I swam. Eyes open, mindful of any exposed body parts that might be dangling in my path. At the other side of the pool, I came up for air, and right before me was a rather plump, elderly couple sitting on the edge, minding their own business. I turned around, took a deep breath and headed underwater back to the other end, where I surfaced only to find myself, God help me, looking into, God help me, the nether regions of a beautiful woman sitting with her legs, God help me, apart. And then…well…it happened. The "e" word. Right there, in the pool. Well, let's just say I had no choice but to swim back (now with the aid of a rudder) toward that plump, elderly couple whose very presence, God bless them…humbled me.

A CALL HOME:

"Are you naked right now, Daddy?"

"No, Sari. Can I please speak to Mommy?"

"Okay."

"Thanks, honey."

"Hey Dad, you take any pictures of the naked folks?"

"No, Adam. Can I please speak to Mommy?"

"Okay."

"Thanks, kiddo."

"Dad?"

"Hi, Lindsay."

"Dad, when you come home, could you limp in front of my friends? The way you would if you actually had minor back surgery?"

"Fine. Can I please speak to Mommy?"

"Okay."

"Thanks, sweetheart."

"Hello?"

"Robin?"

"Yeah?"

"Could you drive out here?"

"When?"

"Now."

"Now?"

"Please?"

"Why?"

"Because I'm hornier than a toad."

"Alan, the kids have school tomorrow."

"Robin, I was around naked people all day, and now it's night, and I'm alone, and I'm ready to burst."

"Alan—"

"Please. It's only a two-hour drive. You can come out, stay seven minutes, then turn around and go home."

"You gotta be kidding."

"You're right. Six minutes."

I hung up, got undressed, went outside and was aware of the fact I had never done those things in exactly that order before.

The Terra Cotta Inn doesn't have a restaurant. (If it did, I wondered, would the chef have to wear two hair nets?) But meals ordered in arrive in no time, as the delivery boys from all the local restaurants race through the streets so they can get to see the home where the naked people roam.

I heard voices and walked in their direction. Much to my surprise, I now had no inhibitions about my nudity. Sure, I was conscious of it, but there I was. Under the stars. Four couples. And me. At a naked pizza party. A couple from L.A. whose children knew where they'd gone for the week-end but weren't told about the clothes part; a middle-aged

CEO from Michigan and his wife of 27 years; a kindergarten teacher and her husband, a retired cop, who've been coming to places like this since 1987; a couple from San Diego, both attorneys and both 32; and me.

I realized I liked these naked people. They were without pretense in addition to being without clothing. So the next morning, when I saw a number of them pass my window holding coffee mugs and doughnuts, I took off my bathrobe and dashed outside to join them. Not only did I spend the entire morning naked, but, by noon, I found the very concept of clothing an absurd one.

A CALL TO A FRIEND:

"Garry, it's Alan. Look, I'm calling because I just felt the need to tell someone that I'm forty-four years old, and about an hour ago, for the first time in my life, I put suntan lotion on my ass. I'll explain later. Bye."

What else can I say other than that I was now one of them? I swam naked. I read Christopher Darden's *In Contempt* naked. I ate a chef's salad naked. I played naked Foosball. I started using my laptop for reasons other than to just cover my lap. And I was quickly becoming more and more intoxicated with my new-found freedom.

"Hi, Tom."

"Hi, Alan. Where you headed?"

"Carl's Jr. The one on Palm Canyon. Want anything?"

"No, thanks."

"Catch you later, Tom."

"Alan?"

"Yeah?"

"Do you think you should put some pants on?"

"What for?"

"Well, the Palm Springs police have rules when it comes to naked men and fast food chains."

"What about the drive-thru?"

"Also the drive-thru."

"Those bastards."

ANOTHER CALL HOME:

"Well, then how about taking a plane?"

"Alan…"

"I'm serious, Robin. The airport's only a few miles from here and—"

"But you're coming home tomorrow."

"Exactly. So I say fly out in the morning, I'll pick you up, bring you here, then we'll drive back to L.A. together."

"We'll see."

"Really?"

"Yeah, yeah."

"Great, because I really want to you to see this place and meet my new friends."

"Jesus…"

"Hey, guess what? Remember when I told you that years ago, this place was where President Kennedy and Marilyn Monroe used to come together?"

"Yeah…?"

"Well, local legend has it they used to stay in room 34, and I went in there today."

"Yeah…?"

"Naked."

"Yeah…?"

"So think about it, Robin. This very afternoon, I was naked in the same exact room that a president and Marilyn Monroe were naked in."

"Yeah...?"

"So the way I see it, in some strange, mysterical way, this afternoon I had sex with..."

"Here, speak to the kids."

"What kids?"

Alan Zweibel has received five Emmys, six Ace and three Writer's Guild Awards for his work in television, which includes Saturday Night Live, *PBS's* Great Performances, *and* It's Garry Shandling's Show. Bunny Bunny, *a stage play that he adapted from his book* Bunny Bunny: Gilda Radner—A Sort of Love Story, *opened in New York to rave reviews. He and his wife Robin have three children.*

*

In Thailand, my fashionable traveling companion and I each bought a sarong, and she taught me how to wrap it.

"It feels precarious," I said.

"Oh, no," she assured me. "If you tie it right, it can't fall off."

Fortunately, it happened to her, not me. Unfortunately it happened in the lobby of a Bangkok hotel. Fortunately, she was wearing a bathing suit underneath it. Unfortunately, it was a black bikini. Fortunately, she was far from home and didn't know a soul in the room.

—Sophia Dembling, "To Err is Humorous,"
The Dallas Morning News

✦ ✱ ✦

Failing to Learn Japanese in Only Five Minutes

If you can figure out how to order a beer,
your language skills are just fine.

THE WAY I ATTEMPTED TO LEARN JAPANESE WAS BY READ-ING a book called *Japanese at a Glance* in the plane from San Francisco to Tokyo. This is not the method recommended by experts. The method recommended by experts is to be born as a Japanese baby and raised by a Japanese family, in Japan.

And even then it's not easy. Learning to *speak* Japanese isn't so bad, but learning to *read* it is insanely difficult. Start with the fact that, for some malevolent reason, the Japanese use *four different systems,* which are often intermixed, in addition to characters sometimes arranged vertically, in which case you read right to left, but sometimes arranged horizontally, in which case you read left to right. (I might have gotten some of this wrong, but, trust me, there's no way you'd be able to tell.) Also sometimes there's a mixture of horizontal and ver-tical writing, using several different character systems.

That's not the hard part. The hard part is that the major Japanese writing system consists of—why not?—*Chinese* characters, which represent words, not sounds. So for each word, you need a different character, which means to be even moderately literate you have to memorize thousands and thousands of characters. This wouldn't be so bad if the characters looked like what they're supposed to represent. But the Japanese/Chinese characters don't look anything like the concepts they're supposed to represent....

And *every one of those marks is important.* If you put one teensy little line in there wrong, you could change the entire meaning of the character, from something like "man holding broom" to "sex with ostriches."

Sometimes it seems as though the whole point

> J apanese Prime Minister
> Tomiichi Murayama
> apologized for Japan's part
> in World War II.... However,
> he still hasn't mentioned
> anything about karaoke.
>
> ◆
>
> —David Letterman

of the Japanese writing system is to keep non-Japanese people from understanding what the hell is going on. The only Westerner I met in Japan who had actually learned to read Chinese/Japanese characters was Tom Reid, who works for *The Washington Post.* He was always trying to explain it to me. He'd write down something, then he'd say, "OK, this character means 'library infested with vermin.' See, this line here"—*here he points to a line that appears identical to all the other lines*—"looks like a tree root, right? And books are the root of knowledge, right? Get it? And this line"—*he points to another random line*—"looks like the whisker of a rat, right? You see it, right? RIGHT?"

I'd always say that yes, I thought I saw it, although what I really thought was that Tom had spent too many hours studying rats' whiskers.

So I never even tried to learn the written language. I sincerely did intend to learn to speak some Japanese before we went over there, but, because of a lot of other things I had to do to prepare for the trip, it turned out that the only concrete linguistic effort I made was to go with my son to a Benihana of Tokyo restaurant in Miami. We thought maybe we could pick up some useful phrases from the waiter, who came out and prepared our steak right in front of us by assaulting it violently with sharp implements and hurling it around the griddle, as though concerned that it might suddenly come to life and attack the patrons. But it turned out that he was Cuban, and the only Japanese expression he knew was the sound you make when you strike a potentially dangerous steak.

So I ended up attempting to learn Japanese on the flight over. I had plenty of time, because flying from the United States to Tokyo takes approximately as long as law school. But the flight is not so bad when you do it the way we did it, namely, first class on Japan Air Lines, with Random House paying for it. This is definitely the way you should do it, if you ever go to Japan. Just tell your travel professional, "I'd like to fly first class, and send the bill to Random House." Don't mention my name....

Before I fell asleep, I was able to devote nearly an hour to the study of the Japanese language. My ultimate goal was to learn how to say "I do not speak Japanese" in fluent Japanese, but I decided to start with "Thank you." According to *Japanese at a Glance,* the way you say this is:

(DOH-moh ah-REE gah-toh)

For some reason—again, it could have been the wine—I found this almost impossible to remember. I tried practicing on the cabin attendants, who continued to come around every few minutes with complimentary items.

"DI-moh ah-bli-GA-toh," I would say.

Or: "DE-mi AL-le-GRET-oh."

Or: "DA-moh o-RE-go-noh."

All of these seemed to work pretty well, but I think the cabin attendants were just being polite. I was worried about how I'd do with regular Japanese civilians, especially in light of the following stern warning from *Japanese at a Glance:*

Take long vowels seriously; pronouncing a long vowel incorrectly can result in a different word, or even an unintelligible one.

So I tried hard to take my long vowels seriously. The last thing I wanted was to try to thank a bellhop and instead, because of a vowel problem, ask for his hand in marriage. After a solid hour I was still not at all confident in my "Thank you," and most of the other phrases in *Japanese at a Glance* were even worse. It was as if they had been cranked out by the Random Syllable Generator. The harder I tried to concentrate, the more confusing the phrases became, until they all looked like this:

Hello (formal): Wa-SO-hah-na-GO-ma-na-SO-la-ti-DOH
Hello (informal): Hah-to-RAH-ma-ka-NYAH-nyah-nyah
Hello (during rain): Ko-rah-na-ma-NAY-ah-MOO-baaaa

The result of this language-training program was that I arrived in Tokyo speaking Japanese at essentially the same fluency level as cement. I never did get much better while we were there. The only word I became really good at saying was "beer," which is pronounced "bee-roo," unless you want a big beer, in which case it is pronounced "BIG bee-roo."

Dave Barry has written quite a few books, including Dave Barry's Guide to Guys, Dave Barry Slept Here, Dave Barry's Greatest Hits, Dave Barry Turns Forty, *and most recently,* Dave Barry is from Mars and Venus. *Notice a title theme here?*

*

Proper German has that "chainsaw cutting through a backed-up septic tank" sound to it, much like Nirvana without the long hair.

—Chris Harris, *Don't Go Europe*

* * *

Jugo Especial

The author cooks up a Peruvian
recipe for revenge.

DURING A TRIP TO PERU, MY BOYFRIEND FILIP AND I WOULD make morning trips to the juice section of the Cuzco market for apple-carrot juice at Eufemia's juice stand. It was, I thought at the time, a cute little romantic ritual that left our lips stained orange for the rest of the day. Eufemia was a smiley gold-toothed young woman who would always, in good humor, try to sell us more than we could drink. "Gringos! For you today special! *¡Jugo Especial!*"

"What's that?" Filip played along.

"All the fruits you see here, plus beet, alfalfa, molasses, beer! And because you are good customers, special price. Five dollar."

"Thanks Eufemia," said Filip. "But it's out of my price range."

"Your boyfriend. He stingy," she informed me. We had a laugh over that one and said we'd save up our money for next time.

A few days later, I went in by myself as Filip was off climbing some mountain that didn't interest me. Eufemia would not accept my usual order of apple-carrot juice.

"Today you try *Jugo Especial,*" she ordered. "You no pay. You tell boyfriend I not stingy." She raised her eyebrow for emphasis.

So when Filip got back I passed on Eufemia's message. He didn't take it with the humor I would've expected. "Screw that hag anyway. I'm not going to her anymore."

As I myself was unhindered by a ridiculous sense of masculine pride, I continued visiting Eufemia. She did, after all, make the best juice in Cuzco. One morning, a week later, she and I were gossiping about the blossoming romance between one of the poultry salesmen and her sister while she shoved apples through the juicer.

"Eufemia!" whispered the lady who owned the neighboring juice stand, "Isn't that the gringa whose boyfriend comes in with that blond girl and orders *Jugo Especial* everyday?"

Eufemia whispered back something to the effect of, "Yeah, it's also the gringa who understands Spanish perfectly, thank you very much."

Meanwhile, my face was the color of the beets Eufemia was now grating as I realized that the entire juice section of the Cuzco market knew my boyfriend was cheating on me before I did.

Eufemia apologized, saying she had tried subtly to warn me. "I guess you no want more *Jugo Especial,*" she mumbled dejectedly. I thanked her anyway and told her not to worry. I was just going to head over to the butcher's section, I said.

"*Eso!*" she cheered me on.

I couldn't have timed my visit more perfectly. There, at the entrance to the beef tables was a sight that warmed my recently dumped, women's college graduate heart: two little girls selling raw testicles. They waved me over.

"Well girls, what have we here?"

"Huevos, son ricos!" Testicles. They're good.

The girls were so enthusiastic I had to buy a pair. When I met up with Filip again it was almost dinner time. He seemed cheerful and had been out visiting the ruins, he claimed. Did I want dinner?

"I'm cooking dinner here, sweetie." I led him in to the hostel's kitchen, enjoying the horrified look on his face when he saw what I was preparing.

"What's that?"

"Testicles dipped in paprika and breadcrumbs and fried in butter. Then I thought we might have some *jugo especial* to go with it...."

Lara Naaman is currently breaking hearts as a cocktail waitress in Houston, Texas, while working on a collection of short stories about South American street food. Men often find her beauty, intelligence, and culinary abilities intimidating.

*

Lara's Just-Been-Dumped Fried Testicles

2 bull's testicles
2 eggs
½ cup bread crumbs
¼ cup grated Parmesan cheese
¼ stick of butter
paprika to taste

Clean the testicles well. In a bowl, beat two eggs together and set aside. In another bowl, mix the Parmesan and bread crumbs. Dip the testicles in the egg, then pass through the bread crumb mixture. In a frying pan, melt the butter and add the coated testicles. Sprinkle liberally with paprika and fry until golden brown.

* * *

Under the Spell of a Witch Doctor

To get permission to head up the Congo River, a cleansing is required.

THE WITCH DOCTOR CURSES. NO ONE TOLD HIM IT WAS AN American coming for the cure. His black eyes bore into mine, probing for something deep inside me. Bright-colored plastic toothpicks pierce his earlobes, and a string of wooden fetishes bounce menacingly across his chest.

"Can you help?" Ambroise, my guide, challenges.

The witch doctor, Fortunado, winces and moves to the left, until our shadows no longer cross. He mumbles something inaudible and shakes his head.

"He has brought money," Ambroise offers as I pull out a wad of West African francs.

The witch doctor surveys me again. After a moment he announces that I'm dirty and that my stink offends the gods, but if I'm willing to pay the price, he will cleanse me of evil. As I hold out the cash, he's careful not to touch my hand. He nods after counting the bills.

"*Déshabillez!*" the witch doctor barks.

Off come my shoes and socks, but not fast enough.

"Vite! Vite!" He doesn't have all day. People all over the Congo await him. He has potions to concoct and spells to cast.

Grabbing the front of my shirt, he repeats in French, "To skin…to skin." For good measure, he kicks my shoes across the courtyard.

"Hurry, you're pissing him off," Ambroise hisses.

I've been in Brazzaville for over a month now, and I'm beginning to wonder if I'll ever be allowed beyond its limits. Congolese officials have been generous with their coffee and croissants, but not with their travel permits. My proposed destination, Lake Télé, fabled home of the supreme jungle deity, Mokele-Mbembe, is off-limits to foreigners without a special pass.

"Wear yourself naked," the witch doctor insists and gestures feverishly at my underwear. Reluctant, I thumb the elastic waistband, recalling how I arrived at this odd situation.

Yesterday, after a particularly long and unproductive meeting with government officials, Ambroise concluded that my approach was all wrong. I must first beseech Mokele-Mbembe and then petition the government for permission to visit Lake Télé.

"God before man," Ambroise insisted. "And to reach Mokele-Mbembe you must be cleansed…. It's the only way."

A small group of men has gathered in the courtyard. The witch doctor scowls as Ambroise urges, "Do it…. Come on, do it."

I suppose a few minutes of public nudity here in the dust of the Bacongo district, miles from my hotel, won't damage my reputation any further.

"Now we will begin." The witch doctor hurls my boxer shorts into the air.

He signals to Ambroise, and the two of them vanish into

the witch doctor's house, leaving me stark naked to the gawking crowd. A *mundélé,* or white man, let alone his genitals, is a rare sight in this neighborhood, and more and more men trickle into the courtyard fenced by a hodgepodge of mud bricks and stones.

I seek the shade and lean against a wall, trying to ignore the wide eyes staring at me. A mongrel trots over for a quick sniff and attempts to mount my leg. A kind gentleman calls the dog and boots it into the street.

Voices are coming from inside the house, but the words are muffled by drawn curtains imprinted with portraits of President Denis Sassou-Nguesso, the Maoist who rose to power in 1979. The talking continues, seconds tick by like hours, and my patience expires. I poke my head through the doorway, interrupting the clink of glasses. Ambroise and Fortunado are sitting comfortably at a table sipping whiskey.

"A toast to a successful cleansing." Ambroise hoists his glass.

"*Oui.*" The witch doctor tosses back his drink and quickly refills his tumbler.

Drawing by Wiley; © 1993 Washington Post Writers Group. Reprinted with permission.

I turn on my heels with a loud harumph and storm back to the courtyard. The curious onlookers retreat to a safe distance as one agitated stranger scrambles for his clothes. The witch doctor bursts from the house and snatches the shirt from my hand. He waves a Fanta bottle filled with a thick, golden liquid.

"Regardez!" He jiggles the bottle.

Intrigued, I watch as he holds it up to the sun. Scores of insects are suspended in the amber goo, and he seems to be clicking his tongue at each one. He plucks a toothpick form his earlobe and jabs it into the neck of the bottle. Then a curious silence ensues. I wonder if the insects convey some cosmic meaning, a horoscope perhaps.

"Are the signs good?" I ask, eager to learn my lot.

"Silence!"

I have had Hindus predict the future from my shadow, and Tibetan lamas have divined my fate from blades of grass tossed in the air, but this oracle of insects is new to me. Most soothsayers in this area rely on a divining board sprinkled with sand; the believer shakes the board, and the resulting lines are interpreted by an Ife-trained fortuneteller. I look for Ambroise, who is moving through the crowd, proudly telling people that he's the one who has brought the *mundélé*.

"Ambroise! What does the witch doctor see?"

Ambroise questions the priest in Lingala, an ancient Bantu language that has a soft, musical quality, with repetitive vowel sounds and drawn-out f's.

"He sees many colors."

"What?"

He shrugs. "That's what he said…many pretty colors."

At last the witch doctor puts down the Fanta bottle and surrounds it with small rocks and dirt. He returns the tooth-

pick to his left ear and removes his rings and bracelets. He
motions me into the middle of the courtyard, exposing me to
an unblinking equatorial sun. Almost immediately sweat
begins to flow down my body, and I wonder how long it will
be until my pink skin scalds. The sun's withering stare,
Ambroise says, is essential to the cleansing process.

The witch doctor rises on the balls of his feet, stretches his
arms skyward, and begins opening and closing his hands
rhythmically. His eyes shut tight, he gulps mouthfuls of air
to capture energy from the sky gods. Invigorated, he stomps
toward me and exhales an unearthly, high-pitched scream.

"Ambroise," I plead from a puddle of sweat.

"Hush!"

The witch doctor spins like a dervish, whooping as he
revolves. His necklace of fetishes dances to life, eerily ani-
mate. He raises one hand, bows, and, without warning, thrusts
his contorted face into mine. Spittle sprays across my brow
as he howls a painful sound. The crowd gasps in admiration.
The witch doctor then tugs on his necklace and issues a
spine-tingling trill for each fetish; I wonder if these vocal
gymnastics are for the audience or the gods.

Suddenly the witch doctor becomes somber and assumes
a look of intense concentration. He appears to fall into a
trance; his eyes glaze, saliva foams in the corners of his mouth,
liquid runs from his nose, and his limbs twitch spasmodically.

"It's working," Ambroise whispers. The people around
him nod.

The sun is blazing hotter than ever, sapping my resolve.
I can feel my bald pate frying, and a powerful thirst has
seized me.

"Give me my hat."

"No!... You must be naked."

"I don't care. My hat, please."

"Shhhh."

The witch doctor, disturbed by our voices, emerges from his trance and wags a finger. Everything is going well; impatience, however, will sabotage the cleansing. He says he was communicating with the gods and has their ear. Ambroise suggests I think about ice cubes.

A young boy fetches a galvanized bucket from the side of the house. A red liquid sloshes over the rim. The witch doctor mutters an incantation while dipping his fingertips into the bucket. He flicks the liquid at me, splattering my body with crimson dots.

"Doorways for the evil spirits," Ambroise advises.

"Protect yourselves," someone in the crowd warns. Instantly the onlookers start praying, aware that the ousted devils will soon be seeking new homes.

The witch doctor steps back to examine his work and adds a few more dots around my feet and navel. Apparently satisfied, he invokes a new sequence of chants, this time kissing a fetish at the start of each one. I feel myself growing faint as the sweat continues to roll off me. My head and shoulders are the color of boiled lobsters. I groan when Fortunado instructs me to flap my arms like a bird.

"Inhale…exhale…inhale…" he orders.

"Drink the air he has purified. Force the devils out!" Ambroise coaches.

The witch doctor bows toward the sun and claps his hands twice. The crowd cheers as he turns and slaps the tender skin on my back.

"Success!" Ambroise trumpets. "You are clean…no more devils."

I thank the witch doctor and scurry for the shade. He

chases after me and yanks me back into the sunlight. The ceremony is not over.

"Hold on. He must seal you from the new devils trying to get back in."

"What?"

"Silence!" The witch doctor picks up the solar-heated Fanta bottle and positions it directly over my head. With a blurp, the sacred potion plops onto my head, much to the amusement of the crowd. Slowly he spreads the jellied substance over my entire body, methodically working his way down to my toes.

The potion has a noxious odor that stings my nostrils. The stench alone should keep devils away. The crowd swings upwind, pinching their noses and dousing their handkerchiefs with perfume.

"I can hardly breathe!" I gag and shut my eyes, irritated by the goo.

"The potion is very powerful," Ambroise observes.

"What's in it?" A bittersweet taste creeps into my mouth. I can hear Ambroise talking to Fortunado as the liquid oozes between my buttocks.

"He says there are many ingredients. Some are secrets, but he did say crocodile oil and honey and bits of…"

I feel a tickling all over and, opening my eyes, I see that I'm shrouded with insects; flies dine on my torso; honeybees graze on my shoulders; tiny beetles crawl in my pubic hair; millipedes picnic in the shade of my insteps; a queue of black ants is working its way up my right leg. As I move to brush them off, the witch doctor pins my arms.

"Be strong," he says, his hands circling my wrists.

"Stand still," Ambroise adds, "and show the devils how strong you are."

The itching is unbearable. Every winged insect within a half kilometer has picked up the scent and swarmed to this six-foot-two-inch lollipop. I recall reading that the Bateke tribes upriver used a similar method to punish infidelity. An adulterer would be slathered with honey, bound to a tree deep in the rain forest, and left to be eaten piecemeal; supposedly the practice stopped decades ago.

"You should see yourself, *très formidable,*" Ambroise pipes gleefully.

Cloaked with insects, I shimmer in the sunlight, a mosaic of iridescent wings, amethyst bodies, emerald fur, cobalt shells, yellow shields, and glistening eyes. The odor of the rancid potion knots my stomach. In the dust I spot a column of driver ants wending its way toward me; wasps start nibbling in the right crease of my crotch, arching their backs and exposing their stingers in a harvest dance.

"Please, O Holy One," I whine.

He finally releases his grip, saying that it's important for all the insects to

> ───── ☽ ─────
>
> In my hotel in Oslo, the chambermaid each morning left me a packet of something called Bio Tex Blå, a "minipakke for ferie, hybel og weekend," according to the instructions. I spent many happy hours sniffing it and experimenting with it, uncertain whether it was for washing out clothes or gargling or cleaning the toilet bowl. In the end I decided it was for washing out clothes—it worked a treat—but for all I know for the rest of the week everywhere I went in Oslo people were saying to each other, "You know, that man smelled like toilet-bowl cleaner."
>
> ◆
>
> —Bill Bryson, *Neither Here Nor There: Travels in Europe*

return to the gods fat and happy. "You are free of devils....
Now go to the river and wash."

"Follow him." Ambroise points to a boy running out of
the courtyard.

Snatching up my cap and underwear, I streak off, shed-
ding bugs with every step. The young boy leads me down
an unpaved street that dead-ends at the Congo River. He
jumps from boulder to boulder and finally points out a rock
pool close to the river's edge. He hands me a bar of soap and
takes a seat. The crowd from the cleansing has followed and
applauds the witch doctor as he arrives. Fishermen leave
their traps to see what the commotion is all about. The goo
does not scrub off easily; I have to scour my already raw
skin with mud and sand before the soap does any good.
Ambroise stands on the river-bank telling anyone who will
listen that he's my redeemer.

"It took weeks to convince the *mundélé*.... My prayers
worked....Yes, I arranged everything."

Rory Nugent has detailed his outrageous adventures in his books
The Search for the Pink Headed Duck: A Journey into the
Himalayas and Down the Brahmaputra *and* Drums Along the
Congo: On the Trail of Mokele-Mbembe, the Last Living
Dinosaur, *from which this story was excerpted.*

✳

I shuffled the Tarot cards three times, then said my name out loud
three times and handed the cards back to Luna. She fanned them
and instructed me to pick several. After examining the cards, she
rattled off just about every cliché that came to mind. "The world
is your oyster. Your cup of life is overflowing. Don't worry, be
happy." Then, with a totally straight face, she said, "You are spending money on silly things with very little return."

—Doug Lansky, "A Journey to Venice Beach"

JOSEPH O'CONNOR

* * *

An Irishman
in Vurjinny

Who would have thought it was
possible to experience culture
shock in Roanoke?

THAT MONDAY AFTERNOON I TOOK A TAXI OUT TO LA Guardia Airport to catch the flight down to Roanoke, Virginia. The plane was absolutely tiny; it held about twenty passengers including myself, my English neighbour, who insisted on telling me that he was an aspiring actor, and his ego. I was sitting in the front seat, and the stewardess was opposite me. Every time I tried to engage her in conversation old Prince Hamlet beside me would butt in and ask something really intelligent like, "So, is Ireland still part of Britain or what?"

When we got to Roanoke Airport the terminal was almost empty. I wandered up to a security man and asked if there was a bank around, or some other place to change travellers' cheques. He laughed uproariously, as though having such a facility in an airport would be like having a condom machine in a convent. He then directed me to a shop where, he said, the assistant might be able to help me.

The shop was one of those places you only see in airports, where they sell individual tampons and packs of anti-travel

29

sickness pills and big fat books which tell you how to become a millionaire without ever having to work for it. I asked the girl behind the counter if she could change my cheque for me. An anxious look invaded her face. She looked over her shoulder even though there was nobody there. "If you could buy somethin'," she said, "it'd make things a whole lot easier, sugar."

I told her I really didn't want to buy anything very expensive, but she said that would be all right, as long as I bought something. So I bought a postcard of the sun setting over a lake and handed her a hundred-dollar travellers' cheque. She handed me back ninety-nine dollars and seventy-five cents.

"You come back now," she beamed, and I assured that I would.

The airport lobby featured a large plastic display unit divided into panels. Each panel featured a faded colour photograph of a local hotel with a telephone number underneath. This was great, I thought, as I stepped up to it full of eager anticipation. Sadly, however, most of the numbers seemed to have been disconnected. The few hotels with functioning phone numbers were all full. I wondered what to do.

Outside on the rank there were no taxis, and the place seemed pretty dead. I went back into the lobby and asked a man on crutches if he knew where I could find a hotel. He didn't. I hung around for almost an hour waiting for a taxi but none showed up. It was getting late and dark now and I didn't fancy a night in Roanoke Airport. So I wandered back into the building again, determined to sort myself out. The lobby was full of car-hire stalls, none of which had any staff working behind them. The only counter which was staffed offered a limousine service. It was a bit pricey, but I figured

I had no choice. The woman on duty said one of their drivers would find me a hotel if he had to drive a hundred miles
to do so. I nodded and signed the agreement form. She put
her fingers in her mouth and let out a piercing whistle.
"Driver," she yelled. "Over here."

The man I had seen hobbling along on crutches turned
out to be the only limo driver on duty. I was a little nervous
at the prospect of him conveying me around the back lanes
of Virginia but he grinned and winked and waved one of his
crutches at me and assured me that everything would be "just
fine." He hobbled out to his car and manoeuvered himself
into it. I followed, still feeling apprehensive as I slithered into
the back seat. He insisted on calling me "sir," I noticed, even
though he was old enough to be my grandfather.

"You ever bin dayun sayouth bufaw, suh?" he said, as we
pulled out of the airport.

"Sorry?" I asked.

"Dahn sayouth, suh? Yevah bin in Vurjinny beefowuh?"

What the fuck was he saying to me? Had I ever been in a
virgin before?

We drove down the airport approach road and went on
Interstate 81. The view of the Blue Ridge Mountains at dusk
was simply stunning. If you've never seen them, all I can tell
you is that they really are blue and they really have ridges and
they look the way mountains do on ornamental placemats
but never do in real life. You would have to be made of stone
not to gasp at the Blue Ridge Mountains. Not even the fact
that John Denver once wrote a song about them can dimin-
ish their phenomenal majesty or greatness. We drove on
through downtown Roanoke, Salem, Lafayette, Ironto and
Christiansburg, where we turned off for the road to
Blacksburg and found a motel on the outskirts of the town.

The woman behind the desk was short and friendly. She said she could let me have a room for eighty dollars, and I said OK, that would be fine. She asked whether I wanted smoking or non, so I said smoking, and she nodded. She handed me the key and took my money and told me she hoped I had a real pleasant evening.

I got the elevator to the first floor feeling mighty. Virginia was going to work out well, I felt. But then, as soon as I started feeling good, things started going bad. I walked into the room and almost keeled over, so awful was the stink of stale cigarette smoke. Now, I smoke myself, as I believe I may have mentioned. I smoke rather too much, in fact. But being in this room was like sucking on an exhaust pipe. I opened both windows as wide as I could and switched on the air conditioner. The stench was still appalling. I changed my shirt and went down to the dining room.

There was nobody there. No staff. No diners. Nobody. I selected a table and sat down at it, waiting for something to happen. After about fifteen minutes a waiter came in with a Walkman on his head. He was humming and singing along with the tune, which was, to judge from his high-pitched squeaks and guttural grunts and extreme pelvic thrusts, something in the heavy metal genre. I waved my arms in the air and managed to attract his attention. He took off the Walkman and peered at me as though he had just woken up from an intense dream and was surprised to find me there.

"Any chance of some food?" I asked.

"Weze abayut closed, suh," he said. "We done closed fav meenutes ago."

"I've been sitting here for fifteen minutes," I said.

He shook his head bitterly and said he would see what he could do. I told him a hamburger and French fries would be fine, with a large glass of Coke, if that wasn't too much trouble. He disappeared into the kitchen and ten minutes later reappeared with a burger the size of a watermelon and a basket of bread rolls.

I asked if I could have some butter and he didn't seem to understand me. I repeated the word several times—butter, butter—but he still just grinned and stared at his feet. I then realized that he understood my accent about as much I understood his. This called for something desperate.

"Could I have some budder?" I said.

His eyes lit up. "Why dedden ya jes say thayut, suh," he said.

I congratulated myself for my bravery, but when the butter dish arrived I was kind of sorry I had bothered. There was more hair in the butter dish than there was in the waiter's nostrils and believe me, that means a lot.

After dinner I retired to my room, full of hope that the hideous ashy odour would have abated somewhat. It hadn't. Even though I had left the windows open, and even though there was a gale-force wind howling through the curtains, the room still smelt like a cancerous lung. I took off my clothes and got into bed. The very sheets and pillowcases smelt of to-bacco. It was so disgusting that I couldn't sleep. I got out and tried the other bed. The smell was even

Illiterate? Write today for free help.

♦

—A Classified Ad

worse. I really was tired now. I crawled around the room on all fours, trying to find the one spot in the entire place where the smell wasn't so bad that it would make a skunk's fart seem like Chanel Number 5. I ended up curled on the floor by the wide open window with two pieces of toilet paper jammed into my ears to drown out the noise of the howling wind. Eighty shagging bucks. There's a sucker born every minute.

Next morning I woke up with a pounding headache. Usually I feel like a cigarette first thing in the morning, but today I just buried my face in my pillow and breathed in deeply. Outside, the morning was absolutely beautiful. The sun was glinting over the Blue Ridge Mountains. I decided to walk the few short miles out to Dublin, Virginia.

Close to Blacksburg the land seemed green and lush, but as I walked along the landscape slowly seemed to change. There were still rich pastures and vast meadows in the distance. But now the fields became smaller, and the land looked poorer. There were very few businesses, a couple of ancient sawmills, a few beaten-up stores with dusty advertisements for John Deere agricultural equipment in the windows. The houses got smaller too, their window frames warped and cracked, their paint flaking and blistering.

After a while I got bored with the road, so I walked off the edge and into the woods. What a transformation! The forest was electric with life and colour. Strange purple and reddish flowers grew on the mulchy floor, thick ferns climbed up the trunks of the trees. The smell of the pines was sweet and heavy, like some kind of drug. Some bird with a high-pitched gorgeous song was whistling somewhere far above me where I couldn't see. A spring gurgled beside my feet, turning the earth to rich red mud. I stood very still breathing the sweet straw-scented air deep into my lungs and I have to tell you, I felt happy.

Joseph O'Connor is the author of several books, including The Secret World of the Irish Male *and* Sweet Liberty: Travels in Irish America, *from which this story was excerpted. He lives in Dublin, Ireland.*

∗

You think pilots make fun of those guys who bring them the last ten feet into the terminal with those cone flashlights? Well, thank you, Vasco da Gama. I kited in from Malaysia, you're going to take me the last furlong, Captain Eveready. I hope you don't blow a D-cell. I'd hate to be stuck out here in the Bermuda Tarmac for the rest of my life.

—Dennis Miller, *The Rants*

* * *

The Deep Fried
Potato Bug

I'll have two fried grasshoppers, a raw slug,
and a glass of beer please…

I THOUGHT AFTER THE FEAST OF CHICKEN FEET HERE IN Vientiane, Laos there could be no further gastronomic traumas for me. I'm prepared for anything, you name it. Human flesh? Make mine rare. Cup of blood? Pour me a double, dash of tabasco and a twist. Snakes, snails, puppy dog tails, slugs and guts, and a hundred other things. I'm ready for them all if they are artfully prepared and served with beer.

Now as night follows day, thirst follows heat. As I walked the Mekong River road, I passed people selling coconuts brimming with milk for the thirsty traveler, soda, fruit juice, and even unchilled beer. My God! When it's 90 degrees in the shade and humid to boot, the thought of unchilled beer is almost as bad as no beer at all. I kept walking, until almost hidden in the leafy folds of a giant banyan tree, there on the river bank, I found a watering hole.

It was really little more than a wooden deck, about ten by twenty feet, covered with thatch and tin, but set within the boughs of the banyan. It was a treehouse. The shady limbs of the great tree held the little house in a cool, dark embrace, giving protection from the midday sun while still affording a delicious view of the placid river.

I heard the friendly sizzle of food frying in good oil; that inviting sound that beckons travelers and laborers anywhere. And I heard the clink of ice and the pop of bottle tops. I stepped off the bank and went inside.

"Mistah. Welcome, Mistah," a sarong-clad woman greeted me. "You drink bia, Mistah?"

"You bet!" I said, and took a seat at one of the low tables near the far railing so as to have the best view of the river.

The lady served me a cold one, and it foamed down my throat in icy relief. I slowly sipped the second one, and as I did I noticed a girl of about sixteen sitting across the deck and engaged in some household activity that looked like it might be stringing beans, and so I assumed it was. I smiled at her and she grinned in return. We exchanged numerous smiles until she finally gathered up her work, brought it over to sit beside me, and resumed her labor.

In a steep-sided bowl she had many dozen live, wriggling, trying-desperately-to-get-out potato bugs. Potato bugs, god-damnit, potato bugs! And she was preparing them as the specialty of the house!

She smiled at me again as she drew another bug from the bowl. Deftly and matter-of-factly, she broke the critter's neck at the back, leaving the head attached, and drew out the contents of his torso. Then she grasped his hind end, cracked the exoskeleton, and slowly drew out his viscera in a long, slimy string.

"You eat?" she asked, holding the carcass up to my face. It twitched.

"Oh," says I, "I eat anything, sure."

"You want?" she offered.

"Uh…. Me no hungry. Okay?"

"Okay," she said, and cracked another neck.

Now, I've eaten insects before. Many times. I've eaten red warrior ants in Borneo where the people use them for their lemon/tarragon flavor to season fish. I've enjoyed numerous kinds of larvae, baked, boiled, and roasted in a leaf. Crickets? Jumping jimminy, ate 'em by the pound, roasted and salted like peanuts. And the noble locust, who looks more like his marine cousin the prawn when cooked, has made me a meal. Recommended by both the libidinous Nero and the abstemious John the Baptist, the locust is an excellent dish. But potato bugs! Oh, God, potato bugs! Eeeiiiww! There is nothing redeeming about a potato bug. He is the ugliest, yuckiest creature on Earth. He is the chosen weapon of wanton boys to throw at girls when they want to really gross them out. A potato bug is a six-legged pustule who, if he has any grace, is an offense even to himself! And I ate him.

I ate a whole bunch of him. I wasn't going to, but this French couple walked in and sat down near me. They were clearly shocked at the butchery being practiced by the bug-slaying girl. The Monsieur spoke English and asked me, with great distaste, what the hell was going on with the potato bugs. I explained as he translated to his wife. She blanched. And I mean she blanched real good, too. As though some wanton boy had just thrown one of the beasties at her. Monsieur didn't look any too healthy either, and I decided this was the time to do away with my last food prejudice.

"Madam cook *Ke Lai* for me?" I asked the girl, using the local name for a stinking, rotten potato bug.

"Yes, yes," she assured me. "One kilo?"

"Oh.... What about a dozen to start?"

She called out to Madam and broke another neck, and soon I heard the furious sizzle of deep frying. The Frenchies looked unwell.

Madam set a plate of french-fried potato bugs in front of me. They were all on their backs, their little bug legs sticking up. A small cup of dipping sauce graced the presentation. A shaker of salt sat nearby. I sprinkled some salt on their fried bodies, tossed a pinch over my shoulder, and took a long pull of beer from my bottle. Then I grabbed a bug by the head and popped him in my mouth.

His spiny legs on my tongue felt alive, as though he would scurry down my throat. I bit down and he crunched audibly. The French caught their breath. The girl continued her casual slaughter and smiled.

"Good?" she inquired.

It was good! So help me it was! Mr. Potato Bug tasted and chewed like a shrimp deep-fried in his own shell until the shell

———⟩———

I wondered how Reza, a Muslim, felt about infidel food, but I shouldn't have bothered: food was food to him. I felt bloated from our earlier dinner, but he acted as if this were the first meal he'd seen in months. As he attacked a haunch of the mangled carcass, I said, "Didn't think you ate pork, Reza?"

He froze, meat and bones splayed from his jaws like a still from *Teenage Cannibals*. His eyeballs peered down at the creature diving into his gullet.

"Just kidding."

♦

—Paul William Roberts, *In Search of the Birth of Jesus: The Real Journey of the Magi* becomes crisp and edible and its flavor permeates the meat. If I were a blind man you might have fooled me into thinking I was eating crustaceans.

"They're not bad," I said to the Gallic duo, and I crunched a few more as they watched in morbid fascination. Then I handed one to Monsieur and said, "Go ahead. Be a man, ha ha!"

I thought about wantonly throwing one at the little woman, but I restrained my boyish self. The challenge I had thrown down to the Frenchman was of the highest masculine order. The simple issuance of it effectively impugned his manhood in the now testosterone-charged air. Frenchy was in a fix: on the one hand, he didn't want to eat a bug—who could blame him?—but on the other, he would be damned among males as a wuss (at least in his own mind) if he refused the awful summons. And he would be doubly damned, as his humiliation would take place in front of girls. He sat upon the razor's edge, but I had faith in him. A Frenchman may be a cultural chauvinist with effeminate gestures, but he is no wuss. He can be a pain in the ass, look lengthily down his nose and denounce things American as he consumes his Big Mac and Coke, but he makes an art of accepting the challenge. Melville shows us the cannibal harpooner Queequeg reaching across the table for beefsteaks with the shaft of his harpoon, but while outlandish, it was a thing done with grace for, he tells us, Queequeg did it *coolly*, and a thing done coolly, he writes, is a thing done with grace.

I saw the hot revulsion in the Frenchman's face begin to cool as he girded his gastronomic loins for the culinary duel. A tremble I had noticed in his hand was visibly abating. His wife looked daggers at me. In the hush, the bug girl audibly broke another neck. In the breathless silence, we could just hear the sound of the guts being drawn out in a long little slurp. My adversary hesitated. A part of me wanted to see him humbled, cast out, bear the mark of shame, be driven east of Eden and all that. But the better part of me would not see my fellow done so cruelly.

"Go ahead," I told him. "High protein, low cholesterol, no tropical oils. Lightly salted. And the sauce is piquant without being overpowering."

He took the proffered bug and boldly chewed it, savoring its shrimp-like taste. We exchanged that special masculine glance that is the gastronomic equivalent of the ancient warrior's arm clasp, a glance that says "Hail, thou bold fellow, and bon appetit!" The missus glanced at her husband in a way that said he would surely be a happy horseman that night.

Frenchy and I ate several bugs together. My work done, I paid the tab and tipped the bug girl. She wiped her gutsy hands and received it gracefully. On my way out I paused, turned and shot Frenchy a sort of half salute, which he returned. I think his wife gave me the finger. But it was subtly done—coolly, I might even say.

Once outside, I saw that the sun was dropping low to touch the horizon and set the waters of the Mekong ablaze with red-gold. I ambled down the dusty river road, a full belly and a full heart, knowing that I had dined, and done, well. *I wonder what tomorrow holds for me*, I mused, *in a world of infinite gastronomic diversity.* Who can say? Not I. But I can say this: A potato bug, artfully prepared and tastefully presented, is still a goddamn, gross, ugly, disgusting potato bug, and I'll never eat another one again! Ptooui!

Richard Sterling is the editor of the award-winning Travelers' Tales Food: A Taste of the Road, *and author of* The Eclectic

Gourmet Guide to San Francisco *and* The Fearless Diner: Tips & Wisdom for Eating Around the World. *He has sampled morsels on every continent and most of them have stayed down.*

✳

I was on a cross country flight, seated by the window. There were three of us in this row. A young woman in her twenties, somewhat shy, somewhat slender, was in the middle. My body was overflowing my seat. The man on the aisle seemed to be doing the same thing. We both seemed to be trying to control our horizontality, in deference to the gazelle between the walruses, but this was difficult and tiring during a six-hour flight. No one spoke. A tensely muffled state existed between the three of us. I rehearsed and planned my coughs. Lunch had been served so we were even a little more bloated than before. The last item to eat was a red apple. As my teeth cracked into the apple, a zit of juice lanced out and splat noisily on her right cheek. She flinched as to electricity, but maintained silence. I was astounded in disbelief; part of me was tickled with laughter at the slapstick; part of me was sad and concerned and tender with her awkwardness, my awkwardness, our awkwardness. I thought of apologizing but the soup of static between us was so thick I couldn't find my way through it.

—George V. Wright, Cuisine Sauvage

* ✶ *

Down Jerky Road

All rules change with the scenery.

AMONG THE PLEASURES OF VACATIONS IS THE CHANCE TO escape the grind, see something new, enjoy the buzz of a big city or commune with nature, get closer to your family, or get away from them for a while, refresh, rejuvenate, and regroup.

But one of the best things about vacations is the way all rules change.

The rules of the diet are the first to go. The minute I enter an airport, I want a candy bar. I want it, and I have it.

When I crave candy on an ordinary day, I substitute a bag of pretzels—or yogurt if the snack absolutely must be sweet. (This changes during Girl Scout cookie season, when my office is a minefield of Thin Mints and Do-Si-Dos, which blow all good intentions to smithereens.)

But as there is no such thing as calories in airports, I pass the time waiting to board with M&Ms, Reese's Peanut Butter Cups or a Kit-Kat bar. On vacation, guilt takes a holiday. (And while in the newsstand buying my treat, I pick up a fashion magazine, too—the M&Ms of reading material.

At home, my taste in magazines leans to the literary. On the road, I snack on *Glamour*.)

Then there's the beef jerky phenomenon.

Vacation time—specifically road trips—is the only time I ever eat beef jerky. This is in no small part because beef jerky is displayed alongside every gas-station cash register in the country.

But I visit gas stations at home, too, so why I buy it only on vacation is one of travel's great mysteries. That and the way the contents of my luggage always double from trip's beginning to end. Does dirt really take up that much space?

Road snacks in general walk on the wild side of health. The four basic road-trip food groups: burgers, chips, Fig Newtons (practically health food), and beef jerky.

It doesn't help that the policy of most roadside diners is, "If It Ain't Movin', Fry It!" By the end of a week on the road, my body screams for fresh vegetables.

Of course, getting the full travel experience requires that when in Rome, we eat Roman food. That's why in San Francisco recently, I drank as much wine in five days as I ordinarily drink in five months at home. And a recent trip to West Texas saw me glomming down enough red meat to get myself banned for life from the k.d. lang fan club.

There's no such thing as cholesterol on the road. In a week in West Texas, I ate three chicken-fried steaks, one filet mignon, a couple of burgers, a lamb-chop dinner, and, of course, beef jerky, regular and spicy. Not counting the bacon. And I'm not even counting my daily bacon-and-eggs breakfast

By the end of the trip, my body was so deprived of greenery, I was grazing on garnishes.

Still, I must beg you please, please to remember that if you ever find yourself ordering McDonald's Double Big Mac (*four* all-beef patties, special sauce, etc.), it is time to go home immediately.

Along with dietary rules, certain rules of dress change on the road.

'Fess up—how many of you wear socks more than one time when you're traveling? Don't be ashamed, it's a vacation thing—lots of people do it. As chocolate has no calories on the road, socks don't get dirty.

And though I'm no fashion plate, I do maintain certain aesthetic standards at home. But my favorite travel shoes—a pair of white walking sneakers—are ugly as homemade sin. So sue me, I'd rather be comfortable than fashionable for serious sightseeing.

I know many of you out there also wear ugly shoes on vacation because I've seen them. No big deal. Walk proud. Walk comfortably. Walk ugly. You're on vacation.

I've also learned to live with really bad hair on the road, though heaven knows I try. Harder or softer water, changes in diet and climate and less time to primp usually conspire to make my hair do strange and terrible things. I've learned to avoid mirrors on the road; there's nothing there I care to see.

Just keep telling yourself that you'll never see any of these people again and if you do, they probably won't recognize you with good hair and fashionable shoes, anyway.

I'm sure there are people out there who eat right and dress well while traveling. Frankly, I don't want to hear about it. I'm already awash with guilt over the transgressions of my last trip. That's one of the dubious pleasures of returning home, where all rules again apply.

Pass the steamed broccoli, please.

Sophia Dembling was born and raised in New York City, but at age nineteen discovered life west of the Hudson. Her search for America led her to Texas, where she now lives and writes.

★

Twenty-four-hour room service generally refers to the length of time that it takes for the club sandwich to arrive.

—Fran Lebowitz, *The Fran Lebowitz Reader*

BILL BRYSON

* * *

Bill's Stroll
Through Paris

Dementia stalks the author
in the City of Light.

THE GIRL AT MY TRAVEL AGENCY IN YORKSHIRE, WHOSE
grasp of the geography of the world south of Leeds is a tri-
fle hazy (I once asked her to book me an airplane ticket to
Brussels and she phoned back ten minutes later to say,
"Would that be the Brussels in Belgium, Mr. Bryson?"),
had booked me into a hotel in the 742nd *arrondissement*,
a charmless neighborhood somewhere on the outskirts
of Calais.

The hotel was one of those sterile, modern places that
always put me in mind of a hospital, but at least it didn't have
the curious timer switches that used to be a feature of hotel
hallways in France. These were a revelation to me when I
first arrived from America. All the light switches in the hallways were timed to go off after ten or fifteen seconds, pre-
sumably as an economy measure. This wasn't so bad if your
room was next to the elevator, but if it was very far down the
hall, and hotel hallways in Paris tend to wander around like
an old man with Alzheimer's, you would generally proceed

the last furlong in total blackness, feeling your way along the walls with flattened palms, and invariably colliding scrotally with the corner of a 19th-century oak table put there, evidently, for that purpose. Occasionally, your groping fingers would alight on something soft and hairy, which you would recognize after a moment as another person, and if he or she spoke English, you could exchange tips.

You soon learned to have your key out and to sprint like hell for your room. The trouble was that when eventually you re-emerged, it was to total blackness once more and to a complete and—mark this—*intentional* absence of light switches, and there was nothing to do but stumble straight-armed through the darkness, like Boris Karloff in *The Mummy*, and hope that you weren't about to blunder into a stairwell. And from this I learned one very important lesson: the French do not like us.

On my first trip to Paris, I kept wondering: "Why does everyone hate me so much?" Fresh off the train, I went to the tourist booth at the Gare du Nord, where a severe young woman in a blue uniform looked at me as if I were infectious. "What do you want?" she said, or at least seemed to say.

"I'd like a room, please," I replied, instantly meek.

"Fill this out." She pushed a long form at me. "Not here. Over there." She indicated with a flick of her head a counter for filling out forms, then turned to the next person in line and said: "What do you want?" I was amazed—I came from a place where everyone was friendly, where even funeral home directors told you to have a nice day as you left to bury your grandmother—but I soon learned that everyone in Paris was like that. You would go into a bakery and be greeted by some vast sluglike creature with a look that told you you would never be friends. In halting French you would ask for a small loaf of bread. The woman would give you a long, cold stare and then put a dead beaver on the counter.

"No, no," you would say, hands aflutter, "not a dead beaver. A loaf of bread."

The sluglike creature would stare at you in patent disbelief, then turn to the other customers and address them in French at much too high a speed for you to follow, but the drift of which clearly was that this person here, this American tourist, had come in and asked for a dead beaver and she had given him a dead beaver and now he was saying that he didn't want a dead beaver at all, he wanted a loaf of bread. The other customers would look at you as if you had just tried to fart in their handbags, and you would have no choice but to slink away and console yourself with the thought that in another four days you would be in Brussels and probably able to eat again.

The other thing I have never understood about the French is why they are so ungrateful. I've always felt that since it was us that liberated them—because let's face it, the French

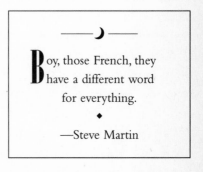

B oy, those French, they have a different word for everything.

♦

—Steve Martin

Army couldn't beat a girls' hockey team—they ought to give all Allied visitors to the country a book of coupons good for free drinks in Pigalle and a ride to the top of the Eiffel Tower. But they never thank you. I have had Belgians and Dutch people hug me around the knees and let me drag them down the street in gratitude to me for liberating their country, even after I have pointed out to them that I wasn't even sperm in

1945, but this is not an experience that is ever likely to happen to anyone in France.

In the evening I strolled the eighteen miles to the Ile de la Cité and Notre-Dame, through the sort of neighborhoods where swarthy men in striped Breton shirts lean on lampposts cleaning their teeth with switchblades and spit between your legs as you pass. But it was a lovely March evening, with just the faintest tang of spring in the air, and once I stumbled onto the Seine, at the Pont de Sully, I was met with perfection. There facing me was the Ile St-Louis, glowing softly and floating on the river like a vision, a medieval hamlet magically preserved in the midst of a modern city. I crossed the bridge and wandered up and down its half dozen shuttered streets, half expecting to find chickens wandering in the road and peasants pushing carts loaded with plague victims, but what I found instead were tiny, swish restaurants and appealing apartments in old buildings.

Hardly anyone was about—a few dawdling customers in the restaurants, a pair of teenaged lovers tonguing each other's uvulas in a doorway, a woman in a fur coat encouraging a poodle to leave *un doodoo* on the pavement. The windows of upstairs apartments were pools of warm light and from the street gave tantalizing glimpses of walls lined with books and windowsills overflowing with pot plants and decorative antiques. It must be wonderful to live on such streets on such an island and to gaze out on such a river. The very luckiest live at the western end, where the streets are busier but the windows overlook Notre-Dame. I cannot imagine tiring of that view, though I suppose in August, when the streets are clogged with tour buses and a million tourists in Bermuda shorts that *shout*, the sense of favored ecstasy may flag.

Even now the streets around the cathedral teemed. It was eight o'clock, but the souvenir shops were still open and doing a brisk trade. I made an unhurried circuit of Notre-Dame and draped myself over a railing by the Seine and watched the *bateaux-mouches* slide by, trimmed with neon, like floating jukeboxes. It was hopelessly romantic....

In the morning I got up early and went for a long walk through the sleeping streets. I love to watch cities wake up and Paris wakes up more abruptly, more startlingly, than any place I know. One minute you have the city to yourself. It's just you and a guy delivering crates of bread, and a couple of droning street-cleaning machines.... Then all at once it's frantic: cars and buses swishing past in sudden abundance, cafés and kiosks opening,

——— ☽ ———

French women, whether pretty or not, all walk around with their noses in the air (and pretty big noses they usually are). I guess this is what's meant by their "sense of style." Where did this sense of style thing get started? The French are a smallish, monkey-looking bunch and not dressed any better, on average, than the citizens of Baltimore. True, you can sit outside in Paris and drink little cups of coffee, but why this is more stylish than sitting inside and drinking large glasses of whiskey I don't know.

♦

—P. J. O'Rourke, *Holidays in Hell*

people flying out of the Metro stations like flocks of startled birds, movement everywhere, thousands and thousands of pairs of hurrying legs.

By eight-thirty Paris is a terrible place for walking. There's too much traffic. A blue haze of uncombusted diesel hangs over every boulevard. I know Baron Haussmann made Paris a grand place to look at, but the man had no concept of traffic flow. At the Arc de Triomphe alone, thirteen roads come together. Can you imagine? I mean to say, here you have a city with the world's most pathologically aggressive drivers— drivers who in other circumstances would be given injections of Valium from syringes the sizes of bicycle pumps and confined to their beds with leather straps—and you give them an open space where they can all try to go in any of thirteen directions at once. Is that asking for trouble or what?

It is interesting to note that the French have had this reputation for bad driving since long before the invention of the internal combustion engine. Even in the 18th century, British travelers to Paris were remarking on what lunatic drivers the French were, on "the astonishing speed with which the carriages and people moved through the streets…. It was not an uncommon sight to see a child run over and probably killed." I quote from Christopher Hibbert's *Grand Tour*, a book whose great virtue is in pointing out that the peoples of Europe have for at least three hundred years been living up to their stereotypes. As long ago as the 16th century, travelers were describing the Italians as voluble, unreliable, and hopelessly corrupt; the Germans as gluttonous; the Swiss as irritatingly officious and tidy; the French as, well, insufferably French.

You also constantly keep coming up against these monumental squares and open spaces that are all but impossible to cross on foot. My wife and I, still mere children, went to Paris on our honeymoon and foolishly tried to cross the Place de la Concorde without first leaving our names at the embassy. Somehow she managed to get to the obelisk in the center, but I was stranded in the midst of a Circus Maximus of killer automobiles, waving weakly to my dear spouse of two days and whimpering softly, while hundreds and hundreds of little buff-colored Renaults were bearing down on me with their drivers all wearing expressions like Jack Nicholson in *Batman*.

It still happens. At the Place de la Bastille, a vast open space dominated on its northeastern side by the glossy new Paris Opera House, I spent three quarters of an hour trying to get from the rue de Lyon to the rue de St Antoine. The problem is that the pedestrian crossing lights have been designed with the clear purpose of leaving the foreign visitor confused, humiliated, and, if all goes according to plan, dead.

This is what happens: you arrive at a square to find all the traffic stopped, but the pedestrian light is red and you know that if you venture so much as a foot off the curb all the cars will surge forward and turn you into a gooey crepe. So you wait. After a minute a blind person comes along and crosses the great cobbled plain without hesitating. Then a 90-year-old lady in a motorized wheelchair trundles past and wobbles across the cobbles to the other side of the square a quarter of a mile away.

You are uncomfortably aware that all the drivers within 50 yards are sitting with moistened lips watching you expectantly, so you pretend that you don't really want to cross the street at all, that actually you've come over here to look at this interesting *fin de siècle* lamppost. After another minute, 150 preschool children are herded across by their teachers, and then the blind man returns from the other direction with two bags of shopping. Finally, the pedestrian light turns green, and you step off the curb and all the cars come charging at you.

And I don't care how paranoid and irrational this sounds; I know for a fact that the people of Paris want me dead.

Eventually, I gave up trying to cross streets in any kind of methodical way and instead just followed whatever route looked least threatening. So it was with some difficulty and not a little surprise that I managed to pick my way by early afternoon to the Louvre, where I found a long, immobile line curled around the entrance courtyard like an abandoned garden hose.

I hovered, undecided whether to join the line, come back later in the faint hope that it would have shrunk, or act like a Frenchman and just jump it. The French were remarkably shameless about this. Every few minutes one would approach the front of the line, pretend to look at his wristwatch, then duck under the barrier and disappear through the door with the people at the front. No one protested, which surprised me. In New York, from where many of these people came, judging by their accents and the bullet holes in their trench coats, the line jumpers would have been seized by the crowd and had their limbs torn from their sockets. Even in London the miscreants would have received a vicious rebuke: "I say, kindly take your place at the back of the line, there's a good fellow"—but here there was not a peep of protest.

I couldn't bring myself to jump the line, but equally I couldn't stand among so much motionless humanity while others were flouting the rule of order and getting away with it. So I passed on, and was rather relieved. The last time I went to the Louvre, in 1972 with Katz [a college friend], it was swarming with visitors and impossible to see anything. The "Mona Lisa" was like a postage stamp viewed through a crowd of heads from another building, and clearly things had not improved since then.

Besides, there was only one painting I especially wanted to see and that was a remarkable 18th-century work, evidently unnoticed by any visitor but me for 200 years among the Louvre's endless corridors. I almost walked past it myself, but something nicked the edge of my gaze and made me turn. It was a painting of two aristocratic ladies, young and not terribly attractive, standing side by side and wearing nothing at all but their jewels and sly smiles. And here's the thing: one of them had her finger plugged casually—one might almost say absentmindedly—into the other's fundament. I can say with some certainty that this was an activity quite unknown in Iowa, even among the wealthy and well traveled, so I went straight off to find Katz, who had cried in dismay fifteen minutes after entering the Louvre, "There's nothing but pictures and shit in this place," and departed moodily for the coffee shop, saying he would wait there for me for 30 minutes and no more. I found him sitting with a Coke, complaining bitterly that he had had to pay two francs for it *and* give a handful of centimes to an old crone for the privilege of peeing in the men's room ("And she watched me the whole time").

"Never mind about that," I said. "You've got to come and see this painting."

"What for?"

"It's very special."

"Why?"

"It just is, believe me. You'll be thanking me in a minute."

"What's so special about it?"

I told him. He refused to believe it. No such picture had ever been painted, and if it had been painted, it wouldn't be hanging in a public gallery. But he came. And the problem was, I couldn't for the life of me find it again. Katz was convinced it was just a cruel joke, designed to waste his time and deprive him of the last two ounces of his Coke, and he spent the rest of the day in a tetchy frame of mind.

Katz was in a tetchy frame of mind throughout most of our stay in Paris. He was convinced everything was out to get him. On the morning of our second day, we were strolling down the Champs-Elysées when a bird shit on his head. "Did you know," I asked a block or two later, "that a bird's shit on your head?"

Instinctively, Katz put a hand to his head, looked at it in horror and with only a mumbled "Wait here," walked with ramrod stiffness in the direction of our hotel. When he reappeared twenty minutes later, he smelled overpoweringly of Brut aftershave and his hair was plastered down like a third-rate Spanish gigolo's, but he appeared to have regained his composure. "I'm ready now," he announced.

Almost immediately another bird shit on his head. Only this time it *really* shit. I don't want to get too graphic, in case you're snacking or anything, but if you can imagine a pot of yogurt upended onto his scalp, I think you'll get the picture. It was running down the sides of his head and everything. "Gosh, Steve, that was one sick bird," I observed helpfully.

Katz was literally speechless. Without a word he turned and walked stiffly back to the hotel, ignoring the turning heads of passersby. He was gone for nearly an hour. When at last he returned, he was wearing a poncho with the hood up. "Just don't say a word," he warned me and strode past. He never really warmed to Paris after that.

Bill Bryson grew up in Iowa and spent twenty years in England, but not because of the food. He is the author of several books, including The Mother Tongue, A Walk in the Woods, *and* Neither Here Nor There: Travels in Europe, *from which this piece was excerpted.*

＊

The Maitre d' fixes you with an intense gaze, and with a sweep of his hand grants permission to leave his exquisite, perfect restaurant. He says only *"Bonsoir, monsieur,"* but his words—so deep, rich (yes, mellifluous)—are a gift, a magnanimous act. You strive to reciprocate, but it comes out too high, absurd: *"Bone-swahr,"* a German dog biscuit which goes skittering across the floor to clatter at the feet of frowning diners. Alas, you are a caveman. You may as well go now to the coat check and ask for your skins and your club and shamble into the night.

—James O'Reilly, "Troglodytes in Gaul,"
Travelers' Tales France

* ✳ *

Dragging the Family to the Magic Kingdom

*Could this be what Walt Disney
had in mind?*

ALAN TAKES MORE VOWS, WHERE TRAVEL IS CONCERNED, than a cloistered nun. His list of Things I Will Never Ever Do Again is by now quite lengthy. But I am resourceful. My tactic is to start with something that really makes his skin crawl—like the four-color brochure on the fourteen-day walk in the foothills of the Himalayas with four gurus and fifteen Sherpa guides sponsored by a travel agency that is a front for Reverend Moon. After that, selling him Disney World was a snap.

He knew we'd have to go to Disney World eventually. It's middle-class America's version of a pilgrimage to Mecca. Every family that can scrape up the cash must make the long and arduous journey to a shrine peopled with more minor deities than the slopes of Mount Olympus: Mickey, Donald, Huey, Louie, and Dewey. With frayed nerves and tattered wallets the faithful stream through the turnstiles of the Magic Kingdom, intent on giving every child his or her birthright: the opportunity to gawk at a six-foot duck in a blue jacket—

the only place you can see that outside of the delirium tremens—throw up on Space Mountain, and run through more coin of the realm than a high-class Bar Mitzvah could account for.

The first thing we realized, as we drove up to the borders of the Magic Kingdom in our rented, super-economy-rate sedan, was that we had left American capitalism and rugged individualism behind. For the next six hours, every move we made would be ordered, planned, and directed, first by perky female voices on the Disney radio network—all we could pick up on the car radio—and then by a series of squeaky clean adolescents who seemed to belong to a family of clones. Disney World may be the world's first working socialist state. Everything is timed, planned, orchestrated. The trains do run on time. "This is what it must have been like in the early days of Mussolini," Alan observed as a clone waved us into our assigned parking spot, Goofy 54. If only Eastern Europe had taken its cue from Walt Disney instead of Karl Marx, the West wouldn't have had a chance. The dummies built the Berlin Wall, when they could have put up Cinderella's castle and had the people battling to get in.

Once inside the park we wandered, mouths agape, down Main Street. If Walt Disney ever read Sinclair Lewis, he never let it show; no dusty, provincial little hicksville here. Main Street was so perfect it took my breath away. The paint fairly shone on the buildings, the window glass sparkled, the gutters were unmarred by as much as a gum wrapper. I began to wonder, could this be what heaven is like? The perfection set my teeth on edge. I began to long for just one shifty-eyed mugger, a lone panhandler with stubbled chin and rancid breath, bumming a dollar for a cup of coffee; one piece of racist graffiti spray-painted on a wall: "Minnie Mouse is a honky." There was none to be found.

Alyssa let out a squeal of delight and began tugging me in the direction of a ride called "Flying Dumbo." I soon found myself standing in a long line, looking up apprehensively as, directly above me, very large Flying Dumbos wearing idiot grins dived out of the sky and then climbed again. As a Dumbo zoomed overhead, my palms began to sweat. I became convinced that this was how I was going to die, on a sticky afternoon in Orlando, Florida. I was going to be fallen upon by a 300-pound Flying Dumbo.

There I would lie, only my sneakered feet protruding from beneath the still grinning, fallen behemoth—just like the scene in *The Wizard of Oz* when Dorothy's house falls on the Wicked Witch. People would snigger reading my obit: "Mother of Two Mashed by Falling Dumbo." I suddenly felt waves of nausea. My daughter smiled up at me. "Isn't this fun!" she piped.

On and on we went, standing in lines, perspiring in the heat being whirled nearly to unconsciousness in a spinning teacup. But it was for the children, no sacrifice too great to bring them joy! At one point Alyssa stood absolutely still, amazement and rapture on her face. "Oh, my God!" she said, her small voice full of absolute wonder. This made it all worthwhile, the plane tickets, getting lost trying to find the motel, getting lost trying to find the car rental place.

"What is it, Alyssa, sweetheart? What do you see?"

She pointed down at her shoes. "Look! Look!" My shoelaces make a perfect figure eight!"

Three hundred dollars for the plane ticket alone. Not to mention the motel, the rental car.

Steven looked up at the sun. "You could sweat your ass off in this place," he said.

I saw the news stories in my mind's eye: "A mother of two was arrested in front of Mr. Toad's Wild Ride today when she apparently went berserk and tried to garrote her children with strings of licorice purchased at the Main Street candy store. Police said she was babbling something incoherent about shoelaces as she was carried off in a straitjacket."

Still, we pushed on. After all, this was once in a lifetime. We still hadn't been through Pirates of the Caribbean. As we approached the entrance, we gave a sigh of relief. No lines in front. We bought our tickets and entered to find ourselves in a winding, narrow corridor built to resemble an ancient dungeon—and the corridor was packed with peo-

> —— ☽ ——
>
> We have noticed something pretty suspicious: every time someone on TV is traveling with American Express Travelers' Cheques, they get robbed.
>
> ◆
>
> —Chris Harris,
> *Don't Go Europe*

ple. Each time we turned a corner there was another corridor—and wall-to-wall humanity. A half-hour passed. Forty-five minutes. Alan is prone to claustrophobia. The crowd began to murmur, the mood turning ugly. Alan's palms began to sweat, he found it hard to breathe.

"A thirty-nine-year-old father of two suffered a coronary today in Pirates of the Caribbean," he muttered. "When he fell, he tumbled into the underground stream and his bloated body floating through the pirate displays immediately became one of the most popular tourist attractions."

A man directly in front of us in line put his ear to the wall. "There's a man on the other side of the wall tapping out a message in Morse code," he announced. "He says he's been in line for four years now." Finally we reached another turn. There before us was…another corridor, another sea of people. Alan peered at a skeleton propped up in a cell off the corridor. "That's Irving Shapiro, a real estate salesman from Perth Amboy. He bought his ticket in 1969."

The grumblings from the crowd grew louder. "How thick could these walls be, anyhow?" someone asked. People can be oppressed for only so long. The spirit of rebellion was brewing. I could see how it would be.

"A group of middle-class American tourists rioted today in the Pirates of the Caribbean attraction. They began a frenzied charge through the corridors screaming revolution-ary slogans, 'Death to Mickey Mouse!' and 'To the guillotine with the lousy dwarfs!' Staff workers in the Disney World attraction had to beat the crowds back with maces and axes from the displays."

Rebellion was averted only by the fact that around the next turn was—the ride. We sailed through pirate battles and emerged, weary, on the other side.

"My shoe hurts," Alyssa whined.

"I'm hungry," Steven whined.

"I'm thirsty," I whined.

Alan hummed his own version of "Cocktails for Two." "In some secluded rendezvous, that's where I'll leave the lot of you."

Alyssa wheedled me into another ride on the Flying Dumbo. Alan looked up at the two of us flying through the air, a beatific smile on his face. "I'm leaving now. You can have the kids and the house and the dog and the cat and the five books of tickets to the rides."

I shook my fist at him. "I'll track you down to the ends of the earth!" I knew how it would go:

"A mother of two went on trial today for hunting down her estranged husband—who had deserted her five years earlier on the Flying Dumbo—and beating him senseless with a Mickey Mouse cap with the ears filled with lead. The judge, who had just returned from Disney World for two weeks with his four kids, ruled it justifiable homicide."

After ten hours, we broke for dinner. Our motel was outside the park. It is easier to get an audience with the Pope than a room inside the Kingdom. We got on the monorail, then on the steamboat, then on the tram that took us back to Goofy 54.

After dinner we decided we had to see the fireworks, so we drove back to the Kingdom, parked in Mickey 73, climbed on the tram that took us to the steamboat which took us across the lake where we stood in line and bought our tickets. Once inside, Alyssa stood still and looked at her shoes.

"What's the matter, sweetheart? Don't you want to see the fireworks?"

"No."

"Don't you like fireworks?"

"Yes."

"Well, Alyssa, what is it that you want?"

"I think I want to throw up."

Caryl Rivers is a journalist, novelist, and professor of journalism at Boston University. This story was excerpted from a book she co-wrote with her husband, For Better, For Worse.

*

Just get on any major highway, and eventually it will dead-end in a Disney parking area large enough to have its own climate, populated by large nomadic families who have been trying to find their cars since the Carter administration.

—Dave Barry, *Dave Barry's Only Travel Guide You'll Ever Need*

Drawing by Wiley; © 1993 Washington Post Writers Group. Reprinted with permission.

* *

A Simian in the Cinema

*An interspecies love affair in
Cameroon sheds light on
the human condition.*

IT IS IMPORTANT IN THIS WORLD TO KNOW TO WHOM ONE is attractive. There was once a particularly touching advertisement for mosquito repellent that began, "One person in two thousand is naturally unattractive to mosquitoes." Alas, sitting on the terrace of the small hotel in Garoua, it was painfully clear that I did not fall into that category. The mosquitoes of that city are determined and vicious, taking time off from relentless procreation only to savage hapless humans. When the doughty female explorer Olive McLeod visited the city just after the turn of the century and had dinner with the German governor, liveried servants placed a domesticated toad at the side of each of the guests to lessen the ravages of the blood-sucking insects.

But mosquitoes do not exhaust my charm. I have a yet stronger effect on monkeys. In England, this attraction remains latent. In Africa, it comes to the fore.

In Dowayoland, I had encountered baboons, possibly the least lovely of simians. Troops of them lived a vocal and arid existence in the rocks beside the path that led to the rain-chief's domain. As I crawled along that sickeningly precipitous track, they would scream and gibber at me and occasionally throw rocks. I suspect now, however, that what I took for rage and aggression was merely a manifestation of frustrated love.

My next encounter with a baboon was when seated on a rock in the middle of a river. In the environs of Ngaoundere was a pleasant spot where the river dropped a clear fifty or sixty feet in a beautiful waterfall. The air was always cool and full of rainbows and dragonflies. A conveniently situated rock made a fine place to sit and bask.

As I sat and contemplated the beauties of nature, I was approached by a baboon. It sat and regarded me with obvious interest from the river bank, exploring its body for fleas in a most immodest fashion. Soon a certain sympathy had developed between us and it daintily picked its way on all fours to where I sat and stared fixedly into my face as if hoping to find I was a long-lost relative. Suddenly it yawned and apparently pointed to something over my head. So great was the sympathy between us that it never occurred to me that this was not a gesture intended for me and I turned round to see what was being pointed at. The baboon, profiting from my distraction, seized my left nipple through the open shirt and began sucking on it vigorously. It did not take this sagacious beast long to realize that this was a fruitless endeavour and we withdrew in mutual embarrassment, the baboon going so far as to spit most offensively. It is possible that this incident was in part responsible for the idea of the missing mastectomy and attendant events.

As I sat on the terrace, quietly swatting mosquitoes, I saw an old friend, Bob, a black American anthropologist. We shared a beer and caught up with each other's news. But out of the corner of my eye, I spotted a movement, at once strange and familiar. It was a monkey swinging through the trees. I knew it was coming for me.

It turned out subsequently that the local zoo had two baby monkeys. I do not know what kind they were, apes, chimpanzees, gorillas, they are all my children. The female of the pair had died. The male had been plunged into deepest mourning. Being an intelligent creature, it had noted that the padlock of its cage was defective. The keeper, in accordance with the regulations that governed his endeavours, had applied in triplicate to the capital for a new padlock. No answer had been received. Any manner of fastening the cage that resisted the monkey's overnight attempts to open it, proved too onerous and inconvenient for the keeper. Any less than final form of closure enabled the monkey to undo the fastening and wander at will during hours of darkness. But it always returned to its cage by morning, the only home it had ever known. A standing arrangement had evolved to the mutual satisfaction of both parties.

In return for being available for public inspection during the day, the monkey was now permitted to engage in nocturnal excursions that had greatly improved its morale. Each evening, it would patiently undo the lock on its door, swing itself into the trees and embark upon a search for suitable company. It has to be confessed that it had sometimes abused this privilege through high spirits but had never failed to report for work in the morning. One of its favorite haunts was the swimming pool of the luxury hotel next door. It delighted in insinuating itself into the changing-huts, plundering the clothes there and retiring to the safety of the trees.

There it would explore the wallets and purses of foreign tourists, raining money, travel documents and doubtless private secrets on the heads of those below, immune to their cries and cajoleries. This had now become an important source of income for the hotel workers who therefore encouraged its visits.

After a moment spent contemplating me from a tree, it dropped to the ground, trotted over to our table and stared at me with the utmost gravity. Over the wall dividing the two establishments drifted howls of rage. Clearly it had just carried out a particularly vehement visitation.

Spotting it, a waiter immediately rushed over to hit it on the head with a rock. This represents a fairly standard Cameroonian response to wildlife. Knowingly, it slid both arms around my neck and slid into my lap, baring green, horribly fetid teeth at its tormentor. Only with the utmost difficulty did I persuade the waiter that it was more reasonable not to hit the monkey—now firmly clamped to me like a limpet mine—so that it would surely savage me nastily, but rather to seek to lure it away with a dish of peanuts. Scowling and muttering, the waiter finally complied, making it abundantly clear that a charge would be made for the nuts. The monkey, however, was not to be parted from me. It began to snore, breathing rank halitosis in my face, disdaining proffered treats. Well-meaning attempts to disentangle its arms produced enraged barks and blaring of surely rabid fangs. Stroking its head brought sighs and grunts of such deep sadness that it would have taken a stonier heart than my own to even seek to discard the beast.

The problem was that Bob and I had set our hearts on a visit to the cinema. Cinemas do not loom large in the accounts of anthropologists yet they are curiously important when in the field. Normally totally inaccessible, they become a focus for feelings of deprivation and nostalgia. Whenever in a town, they must be visited. It does not matter that one knows in advance that the film will be terrible, the soundtrack incomprehensible, the experience full of heat and dust and sweat. It must be done nevertheless. And in town there was a new wonder. An entirely new picture palace had just been opened. It even had seats and a roof. Air-conditioning was promised at any moment. This very evening was one when the film, though doubtless far from new, was not a Kung Fu spectacular or a Muslim epic concerned with the monumental slaying of unbelievers.

Life is full of those actions that seem perfectly reasonable at the time. The logic of a situation is purely a local thing. Many actions, when looked back upon, seem bizarre and inexplicable. "Why don't we just take him along?" suggested Bob. At that particular moment, nothing seemed more natural than that I should take the snoring simian along to the cinema with me. A few tentatively exploratory movements revealed that motion was permitted as long as one hand was kept free to caress the beast. Otherwise, there was more baring of teeth and snarling. It required only slightly more dexterity than that of the average contortionist to insinuate myself into a jacket not designed for a man wearing a monkey and to button it up over the creature. In the damp heat of the evening I felt very warm indeed. Good fortune had provided me with a truck borrowed from my long-

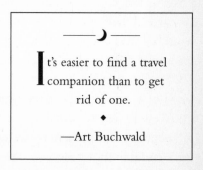

It's easier to find a travel companion than to get rid of one.

◆

—Art Buchwald

suffering friends at the mission. We set off for the cinema, an oddly assorted trio.

It would be nice to be able to report that the film on offer was *King Kong* but it was, I fear, a rather indifferent American comedy about divorce that seemed to fall rather flat among polygamous Muslims.

We queued at the ticket office, various members of the public eyeing my snoring paunch with suspicion. To my great distress, the monkey was detected by the fiery ticket-seller who flared her nostrils at me and called the French manager. I fully expected this to be the end of the matter. The manager would avail himself of the opportunity to vent Gallic rage and point out with ruthless logic all the perfectly valid reasons why simians were not admitted. We should then be shown the door.

Surprisingly, the central issue seemed not to be the admissibility of simians but rather what sort of ticket they required. Bob entered into the spirit of the thing and declared the monkey to be clearly a "minor" and therefore entitled to a reduction. It would not even be occupying a seat. The manager was unwilling to concede the point, fearing perhaps the setting of a precedent. Did he really foresee a stream of people with lions and ant-eaters, refusing payment on this slim pretext? In the end it was agreed that the monkey would be charged at half the rate of the cheapest seat and that we would sit in the least elegant part of the house. I paid up. The monkey slipped back under the coat and began to snore again.

The first part of the programme was not popular. It consisted of a luridly verbose travelogue about holiday cruises in the West Indies. As usual, there were few barriers between members of the audience and conventions of strict silence were certainly not observed. The gentleman beside me, having removed his shoes to ease large splayed feet and unbuttoned his immaculate military uniform to the navel, joked lengthily and repeatedly about my ancestors having given his ancestors free passage on such ships during the slave trade. Bob, a self-aware black American, took such remarks rather ill and a definite atmosphere of tension developed between himself and the military man.

It was at this point that the much-vaunted air-conditioning seemed to leap into action. The temperature dropped steadily until there was a definite chill in the air. It seemed to become more and more hyperactive. Instead of merely mitigating the oppressive heat, it declared war on it. Jets of icy air belched into the room. A sort of miasmic fog seemed to form beneath the screen as the bland French voice prattled on about "getting away from the cold this winter" on a Caribbean cruise.

The military gentleman began buttoning his uniform and struggling back into his boots. Worse yet, the sudden chill penetrated to my simian friend and he poked forth his head to the considerable distress of the lady behind. It was unfortunate that she owned a large, red, shiny handbag. The monkey wanted that handbag desperately and was enraged at that lady's dogged refusal to yield it up. In an attempt to distract the monkey, I bought it a large, red, shiny mango from a passing vendor. Mangoes, however, were strange and unnatural to it. Whatever its normal fare, mangoes were clearly no part of it.

The monkey limited itself to biting the mango into strips and spitting it at members of the audience. Its range was surprisingly great. Bored by the film, they took this in good part, promptly purchased mangoes and began spitting them back at the monkey and—inevitably—at me. The manager, alerted by minions fearful for the décor, hurried up and began threatening eviction. The audience settled back to enjoy a good row as the news came on.

The big story seemed to be a meeting between the President and some unidentifiable Chinese minister dispensing aid. There was the inevitable scene of the President executing a waxy smile into the camera, eyes awkwardly fixed on the lens as he offered the visitor one of the hideous plastic armchairs that were always featured in such scenes. "He should use the aid to buy some new furniture," opined the military man in a loud voice. The audience roared, the news erupted into the national anthem, half the spectators rose, the other half made noises. It was all too much for the monkey. Sated with society, he began to gibber and scream. The audience liked that too. The background of the national anthem made our behavior dangerously close to lèse-majesté. It was the moment to leave, the main film unseen. In a St. Peter-like act of perfidy, Bob remained behind.

We drove back in silence. As I climbed out in front of the hotel, the monkey slipped fluidly to the ground and looked at me a final time as if wondering whether an embrace was too bold on a first date. Deciding against further displays of affection, he shambled off across the yard and swung back into the trees, heading for the zoo.

After all the excitement, I felt quite tired and did not in the least mind missing the main feature at the cinema. However, I did not sleep very well. I had fleas—monkey fleas.

Nigel Barley is a senior anthropologist for the British Museum and spent several years living in Cameroon. His books include Not a Hazardous Sport *and* Ceremony: An Anthropologist's Misadventures in the African Bush, *from which this was excerpted.*

*

I remember on my first trip to Europe going alone to a movie in Copenhagen. In Denmark you are given a ticket for an assigned seat. I went into the cinema and discovered that my ticket directed me to sit beside the only other people in the place, a young couple locked in the sort of passionate embrace associated with dockside reunions at the end of long wars. I could no more have sat beside them than I could have asked to join in—it would have come to much the same thing—so I took a place a few discreet seats away.

People came into the cinema, consulted their tickets and filled the seats around us. By the time the film started there were about thirty of us sitting together in a tight pack in the middle of a vast and otherwise empty auditorium. Two minutes into the movie, a woman laden with shopping made her way with difficulty down my row, stopped beside my seat and told me in a stern voice, full of glottals and indignation, that I was in her place. This caused much play of flashlights among the usherettes and fretful re-examining of tickets by everyone in the vicinity until word got around that I was an American tourist and therefore unable to follow simple seating instructions and I was escorted in some shame back to my assigned place.

—Bill Bryson, *Neither Here Nor There: Travels in Europe*

∗ ✳ ∗

Blinded by the White

It "might have been wiser" not to get lost.

PEOPLE WHO LIVE IN ANTARCTICA DEVELOP AN EYE FOR whites. One day last year, while skidooing the two miles from McMurdo Base to his classroom out on the Ross Ice Shelf, U.S. Antarctic Program survival instructor Bill McCormick spotted a piece of white styrofoam on the snow. You have to admit it's impressive, an ocular achievement akin to spotting a Wheatie in your All-Bran.

McCormick's two-day cold weather survival course is a requirement for new Antarctica arrivals who plan to spend any time in the field. That includes both researchers and support staff, plus the occasional visiting journalist. Students learn how to build emergency snow shelters (igloos, trenches) and operate shortwave radios, and how not to get frostbite or hypothermia doing it.

McCormick, a 48-year-old mountaineering guide from Colorado, is at this moment lecturing on an extremely white weather condition called whiteout. Every fourth or fifth sentence he breaks stride for a swallow of coffee, which he takes black. Whiteouts are snowstorms so trumped-up and incorrigible that ground and air, horizon and sky, are indistinguishable, a colorless, directionless chowder of fog and snow. McCormick has seen people get lost on the 50-foot walk from his classroom to the outhouse. (Another reason to be wary of ice-sheet outhouses: seals occasionally use the opening in the ice as a blowhole. While there's nothing inherently dangerous about a suppositorial blast of hot seal breath, it is, in the words of one shaken veteran, "a disquieting way to start your day.")

McCormick tried for years to come up with an accurate description of what it's like to be in a whiteout. What he finally settled on was being outdoors with a white plastic garbage pail over your head. This gave him an idea. To make his search-and-rescue exercises more challenging for his students (and more entertaining for himself), McCormick requisitioned a stack of white plastic garbage pails.

In this afternoon's search-and-rescue exercise, McCormick is taking the role of the lost victim. A small group of students is given a coil of rope, a sheaf of trail marker flags, garbage pails and instructions to go out and find their instructor without getting lost themselves. That done, McCormick disappears into the almost painful brightness of an Antarctic afternoon. Steve, a carpenter from Colorado, suggests looping the rope around everyone's waist and sweeping back and forth in a line, windshield wiper-style. "What if he's gone beyond the edge of the windshield?" wonders Kevin, a plumber with a Marlboro more or less permanently attached to his face. The class thinks about this for a while. Every now and again, a plaintive "help" issues from somewhere beyond the back door.

Steve is plotting strategy like a high school football coach, filling the chalkboard with arrows and semicircles. "We'll cover from here to here, plant a marker, come back, untie the rope, retrace our steps to here..."

A man who studies nematodes for a living wants to know what the other end of the rope is tied to. Kevin wants to know who died and made Steve king. Someone else is proposing a "sort of backwards, lying-down human pyramid."

"Help..."

"I'll go boil some hot water," says Kevin, as though perhaps McCormick had gone into labor.

Ten minutes pass. McCormick's face appears in the window. It's a face that long ago signed a pact with the sun. "Remember me?" he yells through the glass. "I'm very cold."

Abandoning all hope of an organized rescue effort, the rescuers don garbage pails, loop the rope around themselves and make their way out the door, lurching and groping. Eventually someone trips over McCormick, who is then rolled onto Kevin's parka and dragged across the snow. At some point, probably the point where Kevin trips over the rope and the nematode guy falls over, McCormick has flopped onto his face. "Hey, look," says Kevin. "We suffocated him."

Steve wants to do CPR. Kevin is going through McCormick's pockets. Mount Erebus lounges on the horizon, puffing peaceably.

Back in the classroom, McCormick delivers his critique. The words "might have been wiser" figure prominently. Had this been a real emergency, McCormick would have suffered severe frostbite. "Severe," in this case, is not merely an adjective but an official frostbite category, the other three being Superficial, Deep and Profound. In the Antarctic winter, when windchill bullies the mercury into negative triple digits, a man can get frostbite in the time it takes to find his fly. "Know your layers," says McCormick, who has a way of being superficial and profound at the same time.

In keeping with the experiential nature of the course, dinner takes the form of survival bag rations. All Antarctic flights and field expeditions carry survival bags: canvas duffels with shovels for building snow shelters, camp stoves that can run on plane fuel and a few vacuum-packed backpacking meals to keep your stomach quiet while you freeze. Kevin, tackling dehydrated Turkey Teriyaki, describes the food as "a little preview of death."

It's 9 p.m., time to turn in. The nematode people take the igloo, leaving the rest of the group to share a Scott tent, a bulky teepee-like affair made of bright yellow canvas that blocks most of the wind and some of the sun. (Antarctica in summer presents the uncommon and inadvisable option of tanning while you sleep.) The inside of the tent has an amber glow, like going to sleep with a yellow plastic garbage pail over your head.

Mary Roach has traveled to all seven continents, yet to this day she cannot remember to order special meals. She has written about her travels for Salon, Islands, Condé Nast Traveler, Health, Vogue *and* American Way. *She lives in San Francisco with her husband Ed and their three pieces of luggage.*

*

The beaver's cecum, the part of the intestine that digests hard plant matter, is twenty times longer than the human cecum.

Now that you know that, what do you do?

I haven't the faintest idea. But it's one of the things I've learned during my travels, so I thought I'd pass it along.

—Sophia Dembling, "Travel Facts"

DAVID FOSTER WALLACE

* * *

Shipping Out

A Caribbean cruise becomes cruel
and unusual punishment.

I HAVE NOW SEEN SUCROSE BEACHES AND WATER A VERY bright blue. I have seen an all-red leisure suit with flared lapels. I have smelled suntan lotion spread over 2,100 pounds of hot flesh. I have been addressed as "Mon" in three different nations. I have seen 500 upscale Americans dance the Electric Slide. I have seen sunsets that looked computer-enhanced. I have (very briefly) joined a conga line.

I have seen a lot of really big white ships. I have seen schools of little fish with fins that glow. I have seen and smelled all 145 cats inside the Ernest Hemingway residence in Key West, Florida. I now know the difference between straight bingo and Prize-O. I have seen fluorescent luggage and fluorescent sunglasses and fluorescent pince-nez and over twenty different makes of rubber thong. I have heard steel drums and eaten conch fritters and watched a woman in silver lamé projectile-vomit inside a glass elevator. I have pointed rhythmically at the ceiling to the two-four beat of the same disco music I hated pointing at the ceiling to in 1977.

I have learned that there are actually intensities of blue beyond *very bright* blue. I have eaten more and classier food than I've ever eaten, and done this during a week when I've also learned the difference between "rolling" in heavy seas and "pitching" in heavy seas. I have heard a professional cruise-ship comedian tell folks, without irony, "But seriously." I have seen fuchsia pantsuits and pink sport coats and maroon-and-purple warm-ups and white loafers worn without socks. I have seen professional blackjack dealers so lovely they make you want to clutch your chest. I have heard upscale adult U.S. citizens ask the ship's Guest Relations Desk whether the snorkeling necessitates getting wet, whether the trapshooting will be held outside, whether the crew sleeps on board, and what time the Midnight Buffet is. I now know the precise mixocological difference between a Slippery Nipple and a Fuzzy Navel. I have, in one week, been the object of over 1,500 professional smiles. I have burned and peeled twice. I have met Cruise Staff with the monikers "Mojo Mike," "Cocopuff," and "Dave the Bingo Boy."

I have felt the full clothy weight of a subtropical sky. I have jumped a dozen times at the shattering, flatulence-of-the-gods-like sound of a cruise ship's horn. I have absorbed the basics of mah-jongg and learned how to secure a life jacket over a tuxedo. I have dickered over trinkets with malnourished children. I have learned what it is to become afraid of one's own cabin toilet. I have now heard—and am powerless to describe—reggae elevator music.

I now know the maximum cruising speed of a cruise ship in knots (though I never did get clear on just what a knot is). I have heard people in deck chairs say in all earnestness that it's the humidity rather than the heat. I have seen every type of erythema, pre-melanomic lesion, liver spot, eczema, wart, papular cyst, pot belly, femoral cellulite, varicosity, collagen and silicone enhancement, bad tint, hair transplants that have not taken—i.e., I have seen nearly naked a lot of people I would prefer not to have seen nearly naked. I have acquired and nurtured a potentially lifelong grudge against the ship's hotel manager (whose name was Mr. Dermatis and whom I now and henceforth christen Mr. Dermatitis[1]), an almost reverent respect for my table's waiter, and a searing crush on my cabin steward, Petra, she of the dimples and broad candid brow, who always wore a nurse's starched and rustling whites and smelled of the cedary Norwegian disinfectant she swabbed bathrooms down with, and who cleaned my cabin within a centimeter of its life at least ten times a day but could never be caught in the actual act of cleaning—a figure of magical and abiding charm, and well worth a postcard all her own.

I now know every conceivable rationale for somebody spending more than $3,000 to go on a Caribbean cruise. To be specific: voluntarily and for pay, I underwent a Seven-Night (7NC) Caribbean Cruise on board the m.v. *Zenith* (which no wag could resist immediately rechristening the m.v. *Nadir*), a 47,255-ton ship owned by Celebrity Cruises, Inc., one of the twenty-odd cruise lines that operate out of south Florida and specialize in "Megaships," the floating wedding cakes with occupancies in four figures and engines the size of branch banks.[2] The vessel and facilities were, from

---

[1] Somewhere he'd gotten the impression that I was an investigative journalist and wouldn't let me see the galley, bridge, or staff decks, or interview any of the crew in an on-the-record way, and he wore sunglasses indoors, and epaulets, and kept talking on the phone for long stretches of time in Greek when I was in his office after I'd skipped the karaoke semifinals in the Rendez-Vous Lounge to make a special appointment to see him, and I wish him ill.

what I now understand of the industry's standards, absolutely top-hole. The food was beyond belief, the service unimpeachable, the shore excursions and shipboard activities organized for maximal stimulation down to the tiniest detail. The ship was so clean and white it looked boiled. The western Caribbean's blue varied between baby-blanket and fluorescent; likewise the sky. Temperatures were uterine. The very sun itself seemed preset for our comfort. The crew-to-passenger ratio was 1.2 to 2. It was a Luxury Cruise.

All of the Megalines offer the same basic product—not a service or a set of services but more like a feeling: a blend of relaxation and stimulation, stressless indulgence and frantic tourism, that special mix of servility and condescension that's marketed under configurations of the verb "to pamper." This verb positively studs the Megalines' various brochures: "…as you've never been pampered before," "…to pamper yourself in our Jacuzzis and saunas," "Let us pamper you," "Pamper yourself in the warm zephyrs of the Bahamas." The fact that adult Americans tend to associate the word "pamper" with a certain *other* consumer product is not an

---

[2] Of the Megalines out of south Florida there's also Commodore, Costa, Majesty, Regal, Dolphin, Princess, Royal Caribbean, Renaissance, Royal Cruise Line, Holland America, Cunard, Norwegian Cruise Line, Crystal, and Regency Cruises. Plus the Wal-Mart of the cruise industry, Carnival, which the other lines refer to sometimes as "Carnivore." The present market's various niches—Singles, Old People, Theme, Special Interest, Corporate, Party, Family, Mass-Market, Luxury, Absurd Luxury, Grotesque Luxury— have all pretty much been carved and staked out and are now competed for viciously. The 7NC Megaship cruiser is a genre of ship all its own, like the destroyer. The ships tend to be designed in America, built in Germany, registered out of Liberia, and both captained and owned, for the most part, by Scandinavians and Greeks, which is kind of interesting, since these are the same peoples who have dominated sea travel pretty much forever. Celebrity Cruises is owned by the Chandris Group; the X on their three ships' smokestacks isn't an X but a Greek *chi,* for Chandris, a Greek shipping family so ancient and powerful they apparently regarded Onassis as a punk.

accident, I think, and the connotation is not lost on the mass-market Megalines and their advertisers.

UNDER SAIL

Our horn is genuinely planet-shattering. Departure at 4:30 turns out to be a not untasteful affair of crepe and horns. Each deck has walkways outside, with railings made of really good wood. It's now overcast, and the ocean way below is dull and frothy. Docking and undocking are the two times the Megacruiser's captain actually steers the ship; Captain G. Panagiotakis has now wheeled us around and pointed our snout at the open sea, and we—large and white and clean— are under sail.

The whole first two days and nights are bad weather, with high-pitched winds, heaving seas, spume lashing the port-holes' glass. For forty-plus hours it's more like a North Sea Cruise, and the Celebrity staff goes around looking regretful but not apologetic, and in all fairness it's hard to find a way to blame Celebrity Cruises, Inc. for the weather. The staff keeps urging us to enjoy the view from the railings on the lee side of the *Nadir.* The one other guy who joins me in trying out the non-lee side has his glasses blown off by the gale. I keep waiting to see somebody from the crew wearing the traditional yellow slicker, but no luck. The railing I do most of my contemplative gazing from is on Deck 10, so the sea is way below, slopping and heaving around, so it's a little like looking down into a briskly flushing toilet. No shark fins in view.

In heavy seas, hypochondriacs are kept busy taking their gastric pulse every couple of seconds and wondering whether what they're feeling is maybe the onset of seasickness. Seasickness-wise, though, it turns out that bad weather is sort of like battle: there's no way to know ahead of time how you'll react. A test of the deep and involuntary stuff of a man. I myself turn out not to get seasick. For the whole first rough-sea day, I puzzle over the fact that every other passenger on the m.v. *Nadir* looks to have received identical little weird shaving-cuts behind his or her left ear—which in the case of female passengers seems especially strange—until I learn that these little round Band-Aidish things on everybody's neck are special new super-powered transdermal motion-sickness patches, which apparently nobody with any kind of clue about 7NC Luxury Cruising now leaves home without. A lot of the passengers get seasick anyway, these first two

——— ☽ ———

"A bucket! A pail!" I cried, adding with my last breath, "I'm going to be sick…" Joel stood nodding, his face a mask of concentration. Finally, recalling my younger days as a charades whiz, I tilted my head back and pantomimed a geyser. At this the messman ran off again. I was terrified he'd return with a pair of binoculars, for whale watching, but he reappeared on the double carrying a two-quart sauce pan.

◆

—Jeff Greenwald, *The Size of the World: Once Around Without Leaving the Ground*

howling days. It turns out that a seasick person really does look green, though it's an odd and ghostly green, pasty and toadish, and more than a little corpselike when the seasick person is dressed in formal dinner wear.

For the first two nights, who's feeling seasick and who's not and who's not now but was a little while ago or isn't feeling it yet by thinks it's maybe coming on, etc., is a big topic of conversation at Table 64 in the Five-Star Caravelle Restaurant.[3] Discussing nausea and vomiting while eating intricately prepared gourmet foods doesn't seem to bother anybody. Common suffering and fear of suffering turn out to be a terrific ice-breaker, and ice-breaking is pretty important, because on a 7NC you eat at the same designated table with the same companions all week.

There are seven other people with me at good old Table 64, all from south Florida. Four know one another in private landlocked life and have requested to be at the same table. The other three people are an old couple and their granddaughter, whose name is Mona. I am the only first-time Luxury Cruiser at Table 64. With the conspicuous exception of Mona, I like all my tablemates a lot, and I want to get a description of supper out of the way fast and avoid saying much about them for fear of hurting their feelings by noting any character defects or eccentricities that might seem potentially mean. Besides me, there are five women and two men, and both men are completely silent except on the subjects of golf, business, transdermal motion-sickness prophylaxis, and the legalities of getting stuff through customs. The women carry Table 64's conversational ball. One of the reasons I like all these women (except Mona) so much is that they laugh really hard at my jokes, even lame or very obscure jokes, although they all *sort* of *scream* before they laugh, so that for one excruciating second you can't tell whether they're getting ready to laugh or whether they're seeing something hideous and screamworthy over your shoulder.

---

[3] This is on Deck 7, the serious dining room, and it's never called just "the Caravelle Restaurant" (and never just "the Restaurant")—it's always "the Five-Star Caravelle Restaurant."

My favorite tablemate is Trudy, whose husband is back home managing some sudden crisis at the couple's cellular-phone business and has given his ticket to Alice, their heavy and extremely well-dressed daughter, who is on spring break from Miami U. and who is for some reason very anxious to communicate to me that she has a Serious Boyfriend, whose name is apparently Patrick. Alice's continual assertion of her relationship-status may be a defensive tactic against Trudy, who keeps pulling professionally retouched 4 x 5 glossies of Alice out of her purse and showing them to me with Alice sitting right there, and who, every time Alice mentions Patrick, suffers some sort of weird facial tic or grimace where the canine tooth on one side of her face shows but the other side's doesn't. Trudy is fifty-six and looks—and I mean this in the nicest possible way—rather like Jackie Gleason in drag, and has a particularly loud pre-laugh scream that is a real arrhythmia-producer, and is the one who coerces me into Wednesday night's conga line, and gets me strung out on Snowball Jackpot Bingo. Trudy is also an incredible lay authority on 7NC Luxury Cruises, this being her sixth in a decade; she and her best friend, Esther (thin-faced, subtly ravaged-looking, the distaff part of the couple from Miami), have tales to tell about Carnival, Princess, Crystal, and Cunard too fraught with libel potential to reproduce here.

By midweek it starts to strike me that I have never before been party to such a minute and exacting analysis of the food and service of a meal I am just at that moment eating. Nothing escapes the attention of T and E: the symmetry of the parsley sprigs atop the boiled baby carrots, the consistency of the bread, the flavor and mastication-friendliness of various cuts of meat, the celerity and flambé technique of the various pastry guys in tall white hats who appear tableside when items have to be set on fire (a major percentage of the desserts in the Five-Star Caravelle Restaurant have to be set on fire), and so on. The waiter and busboy keep circling the table, going "Finish? Finish?" while Esther and Trudy have exchanges like:

"Honey you don't look happy with the potatoes. What's the problem?"

"I'm fine. It's fine. Everything's fine."

"Don't lie. Honey with that face who could lie? Frank, am I right? This is a person with a face incapable of lying."

"There's nothing wrong Esther darling, I swear it."

"You're not happy with the conch."

"All right. I have got a problem with the conch."

"Did I tell you? Frank, did I tell her?" [Frank silently probes his ear with pinkie.] "Was I right? Trudy I could tell just by looking you weren't happy."

"I'm fine with the potatoes. It's the conch."

> A luxury liner is really just a bad play surrounded by water.
>
> ◆
>
> —Clive James,
> *Unreliable Memoirs*

"Did I tell you about seasonal fish on ships? What did I tell you?"

"The potatoes are good."

Mona is eighteen. Her grandparents have been taking her on a Luxury Cruise every spring since she was five. Mona always sleeps through both breakfast and lunch and spends all night at the Scorpio Disco and in the Mayfair Casino playing the slots. She is six two if she's an inch. She's going to attend Penn State next fall, because the agreement is that she'll receive a four-wheel-drive vehicle if she goes someplace where there might be snow. She is unabashed in recounting this college-selection criterion. She is an incredibly demanding passenger and diner, but her complaints about slight aesthetic and gustatory imperfections at table lack Trudy and Esther's discernment and come off as simply churlish. Mona is also kind of strange-looking: a body like Brigitte Nielsen or some centerfold on steroids, and above it, framed in resplendent blond hair, the tiny unhappy face of a kind of corrupt doll. Her grandparents, who retire every night right after supper, always make a small ceremony after dessert of handing Mona $100 to "go have some fun" with. This $100 bill is always in one of those little ceremonial bank envelopes that has Franklin's face staring out of a porthole-like window in the front, and written on the envelope in red Magic Marker is always "We Love You, Honey." Mona never once says thank you. She also rolls her eyes at just about everything her grandparents say, a habit that very quickly drives me up the wall.

Mona's special customary gig on 7NC Luxury Cruises is to lie to the waiter and maitre d' and say that Thursday is her birthday, so that at the Formal supper on Thursday she gets bunting and a heart-shaped helium balloon tied to her chair, and her own cake, and pretty much the whole restaurant staff comes out and forms a circle around her and sings to her. Her real birthday, she informs me on Monday, is July 29, and when I quietly observe that July 29 is also the birthday of Benito Mussolini, Mona's grandmother shoots me kind of a death-look, although Mona herself is excited at the coincidence, apparently confusing the names Mussolini and Maserati....

PAMPERED TO DEATH

Celebrity's brochure does not lie or exaggerate, however, in the luxury department, and I now confront the journalistic problem of not being sure how many examples I need to list in order to communicate the atmosphere of sybaritic and nearly insanity-producing pampering on board the m.v. *Nadir.* Take, as one example, the moment right after sailing when I want to go out to Deck 10's port rail for some introductory vista-gazing and thus decide I need some zinc oxide for my peel-prone nose. My zinc oxide's still in my big duffel bag, which at that point is piled with all of Deck 10's other luggage in the little area between the 10-Fore elevator and the 10-Fore staircase while little guys in cadet-blue Celebrity jumpsuits, porters (entirely Lebanese, it seems), are cross-checking the luggage tags with the *Nadir's* passenger list and lugging everything to people's cabins.

So I come out and spot my duffel among the luggage, and I start to grab and haul it out of the towering pile of leather and nylon, think I'll just whisk the bag back to Cabin 1009 myself and root through it and find my zinc oxide. One of the porters sees me starting to grab the bag, though, and he dumps all four of the massive pieces of luggage he's staggering with and leaps to intercept me. At first I'm afraid he thinks I'm some kind of baggage thief and wants to see my claim check or something. But it turns out that what he wants is my duffel: he wants to carry it to 1009 for me. And I, who am about half again this poor little herniated guy's size (as is the duffel bag itself), protest politely, trying to be considerate, saying Don't Fret, Not a Big Deal, Just Need My Good Old Zinc Oxide, I'll Just Get the Big Old Heavy Weather-Stained Sucker Out of Here Myself.

And now a very strange argument ensues, me versus the

Lebanese porter, because, I now understand, I am putting this guy, who barely speaks English, in a terrible kind of sedulous-service double bind, a paradox of pampering: The Passenger's Always Right versus Never Let a Passenger Carry His Own Bag. Clueless at the time about what this poor man is going through, I wave off both his high-pitched protests and his agonized expression as mere servile courtesy, and I extract the duffel and lug it up the hall to 1009 and slather the old beak with zinc oxide and go outside to watch Florida recede cinematically à la F. Conroy.

Only later do I understand what I've done. Only later do I learn that that little Lebanese Deck-10 porter had his head just about chewed off by the (also Lebanese) Deck-10 Head Porter, who had his own head chewed off by the Austrian Chief Steward, who received confirmed reports that a passenger had been seen carrying his own bag up the port hallway of Deck 10 and now demanded a rolling Lebanese head for this clear indication of porterly dereliction, and the Austrian Chief Steward had reported the incident to the ship's officer in the

> ———— ☽ ————
>
> It's very simple, really. You fight your way home, kiss the dog, have a quick beer, go pack a bag or two, grab your bunky, turn off the answering machine, tell the boss your wealthy Aunt Hepzibah just died in Dubuque, and fifteen hours or so later you're lying a couple of feet down the beach from me, snarfing up rays like a dead tarantula and wondering whether to take off your t-shirt or not.
>
> ♦
>
> —Zeke Wigglesworth,
> "The Cook Islands,"
> *San Jose Mercury News*

Guest Relations Department, a Greek guy with Revo shades and a walkie-talkie and epaulets so complex I never did figure out what his rank was; and this high-ranking Greek guy actually came around to 1009 after Saturday's supper to apologize on behalf of practically the entire Chandris shipping line and to assure me that ragged-necked Lebanese heads were even at that moment rolling down various corridors in piacular recompense for my having had to carry my own bag. And even though this Greek officer's English was in lots of ways better than mine, it took me no less than ten minutes to detail the double bind I'd put the porter in—brandishing at relevant moments the actual tube of zinc oxide that had caused the whole snafu—ten or more minutes before I could get enough of a promise from the Greek officer that various chewed-off heads would be reattached and employee records unbesmirched to feel comfortable enough to allow the officer to leave;[4] and the whole incident was incredibly frazzling and despair-fraught, and filled almost half a spiral notebook, and is here recounted in only its barest psychoskeletal outline.

SOME ORGANIZED FUN

2:30 p.m: Now I'm down in Deck 8's Rainbow Room for *"Behind the Scenes." Meet your Cruise Director Scott Peterson and find out what it's really like to work on a cruise ship!* Scott Peterson is a tan guy with tall rigid hair, a high-watt smile, an escargot mustache, and a gleaming Rolex—basically the sort of guy who looks entirely at home in sockless white loafers and a mint-green golf shirt—and is one of my

---

[4] In further retrospect, I think the only thing I really persuaded this Greek officer of was that I was very weird, and possibly unstable, which impression I'm sure was shared with Mr. Dermatitis and combined with that same first night's au-jus-as-shark-bait request to destroy my credibility with Dermatitis before I even got in to see him.

very least favorite Celebrity Cruises employees, though
with Scott Peterson it's a case of mildly enjoyable annoy-
ance rather than the terrified loathing I feel for Mr.
Dermatitis. The very best way to describe Scott Peterson's
demeanor is that it looks like he's constantly posing for a
photograph nobody is taking. He mounts the Rainbow
Room's low brass dais, reverses his chair, sits like a cabaret
singer, and holds forth. There are maybe fifty people at-
tending, and I have to admit that some of them seem to like
Scott Peterson a lot, and to enjoy his talk, a talk that, not
surprisingly, turns out to be more about what it's like to be
Scott Peterson than about what it's like to work on the
good old *Nadir*. Topics covered include where and under
what circumstances Scott Peterson grew up, how Scott
Peterson got interested in cruise ships, how Scott Peterson
and his college roommate got their first jobs together on a
cruise ship, some hilarious booboos in Scott Peterson's first
months on the job, every celebrity Scott Peterson has personally met and shaken the hand of, how much Scott
Peterson loves the people he gets to meet working on a
cruise ship, how much Scott Peterson loves just working on
a cruise ship in general, how Scott Peterson met the future
Mrs. Scott Peterson working on a cruise ship, and how Mrs.
Scott Peterson now works on a different cruise ship and
how challenging it is to sustain an intimate relationship as
warm and in all respects wonderful as that of Mr. and Mrs.
Scott Peterson when you work on different cruise ships and
lay eyes on each other only about every sixth week, except
that now Scott Peterson's grateful to be able to announce
that Mrs. Scott Peterson happens to be on a well-earned vacation and is, as a rare treat, here this week cruising on the
m.v. *Nadir* with him and is, as a matter of fact, right here

with us in the audience today, and wouldn't Mrs. S.P. like to
stand up and take a bow....

3:20 p.m.: *The Nadir Daily* neglects to mention that the
trapshooting is a *competitive* Organized Activity. The charge is
$1 a shot, but you have to purchase your shots in sets of ten,
and there's a large and vaguely gun-shaped plaque for the best
score. I arrive at 8-Aft late; a male *Nadir*ite is already shooting, and several other males have formed a line and are waiting to shoot. The *Nadir's* wake is a big fuzzy V way below the
aft rail. Two sullen Greek NCOs in earmuffs run the show. I
am seventh and last in line. The other guys refer to the tar-
gets as "pigeons," but what they really look like is little dis-
cuses painted the Day-Glo orange of expensive hunting
wear. The orange, I posit, is for ease of visual tracking, and
the color must really help, because the trim bearded guy in
aviator glasses currently shooting is wreaking absolute devas-
tation in the air over the stern.

I assume you already know the basic trapshooting conventions from movies or TV: the lackey at the weird little cata-
pultish device, the bracing and pointing and order to "Pull!,"
the combination thud and *kertwang* of the catapult, the brisk
crack of the weapon, and the midair disintegration of the
luckless pigeon. Everybody in line with me is male, though
there are a number of females in the crowd that's watching
the competition from the 9-Aft balcony above and behind us.

From the line, watching, three things are striking: (a) what
on TV is a brisk crack is here a whooming roar that apparently is what a shotgun really sounds like; (b) trapshooting
looks comparatively easy, because now the stocky older guy
who's replaced the trim bearded guy at the rail is also blow-
ing these little fluorescent plates away one after the other, so
that a steady rain of lumpy orange crud is falling into the

Nadir's wake; (c) a clay pigeon, when shot, undergoes a frighteningly familiar-looking midflight peripeteia—erupting material, changing vector, and plummeting seaward in a corkscrewy way that all eerily recalls footage of the 1986 *Challenger* disaster.

All the shooters who precede me seem to fire with a kind of casual scorn, and all get eight out of ten or above. But it turns out that, of these six guys, three have military-combat backgrounds, another two are L.L. Bean-model-type brothers who spend weeks every year hunting various fast-flying species with their "Pa*pa*" in southern Canada, and the last has got not only his own earmuffs, plus his own shotgun in a special crushed-velvet-lined case, but also his own trapshooting range in his backyard[5] in North Carolina. When it's finally my turn, the earmuffs they give me have somebody else's ear-oil on them and don't fit my head very well. The gun itself is shockingly heavy and stinks of what I'm told is cordite, small pubic spirals of which are still exiting the barrel from the Korea-vet who preceded me and is tied for first with 10/10. The two brothers are the only entrants even near my age; both got scores of 9/10 and are now appraising me coolly from identical prep-school-slouch positions against the starboard rail. The Greek NCOs seem extremely bored. I am handed the heavy gun and told to "be bracing a hip" against the aft rail and then to place the stock of the weapon against, no, not the shoulder of my hold-the-gun arm but the shoulder of my pull-the-trigger arm. (My initial error in this latter regard results in a severely distorted aim that makes the Greek by the catapult do a rather neat drop-and-roll.)

---

[5] !

Let's not spend a lot of time drawing this whole incident out. Let me simply say that, yes, my own trapshooting score was noticeably lower than the other entrant's scores, then simply make a few disinterested observations for the benefit of any novice contemplating trapshooting from a 7NC Megaship, and then we'll move on: (1) A certain level of displayed ineptitude with a firearm will cause everyone who knows anything about firearms to converge on you all at the same time with cautions and advice and handy tips. (2) A lot of the advice in (1) boils down to exhortations to "lead" the launched pigeon, but nobody explains whether this means that the gun's barrel should move across the sky with the pigeon or should instead sort of lie in static ambush along some point in the pigeon's projected path. (3) Whatever a "hair-trigger" is, a shotgun does not have one. (4) If you've never fired a gun before, the urge to close your eyes at the precise moment of concussion is, for all practical purposes, irresistible. (5) The well-known "kick" of a fired shotgun is no misnomer; it knocks you back several steps with your arms pinwheeling wildly for balance, which when you're holding a still-loaded gun results in mass screaming and ducking and then on the next shot a conspicuous thinning of the crowd in the 9-Aft gallery above. Finally, (6), know that an unshot discus's movement against the *vast lapis lazuli* dome of the open ocean's sky is sun-like—i.e., orange and parabolic and right-to-left—and that its disappearance into the sea is edge-first and splashless and sad.

David Foster Wallace is a contributing editor at Harpers, *where a much longer version of this story originally appeared. He is also the author of* Infinite Jest *and* A Supposedly Fun Thing I'll Never Do Again.

I wondered why these passengers ever bothered to disembark, because all Greece was presented to them on the boat, albeit a Greece which exist nowhere else. In the lounge two dancers and a bouzouki band were putting on a performance of folk music.... The audience, mostly Germans and Americans, had no way of knowing if this was how Greek dancing was meant to look, so they applauded with moderate enthusiasm. Afterwards one of the dancers took the microphone and sang "Strangers in the Night." It was my first encounter with Faux Travel, a fabrication designed to ensure that the consumer has all comforts and no surprises.

—David Dale, *The Obsessive Traveller, or, Why I Don't
Steal Towels from Great Hotels Any More*

"*Be patient, Madam. The judging of the funny hats
will resume as soon as we get ashore.*"

PETER MAYLE

. ⁎ .

The Great Goat Race

*Chèvre (goat cheese) will
never taste the same.*

WE HAD FIRST SEEN THE POSTER A WEEK BEFORE, TAPED TO
the window of a *tabac*. There was to be a *Grande Course de
Chèvres* through the streets of Bonnieux, starting from the
Café César. The ten runners and their drivers were listed by
name. There were numerous prizes, bets could be placed,
and, said the poster, animation would be assured by a grand
orchestra. It was clearly going to be a sporting event of some
magnitude, Bonnieux's answer to the Cheltenham Gold Cup
or the Kentucky Derby. We arrived well before the race to
be sure of a good position.

By nine o'clock it was already too hot to wear a watch,
and the terrace in front of the Café César was spilling over
with customers having their breakfast of *tartines* and cold
beer. Against the wall of the steps leading down to the rue
Voltaire, a large woman had established herself at a table,
shaded by a parasol that advertised VÉRITABLE JUS DE FRUIT.
She beamed at us, riffling a book of tickets and rattling a cash
box. She was the official bookmaker, although there was a

man taking off-track bets in the back of the café, and she invited us to try our luck. "Look before you bet," she said. "The runners are down there."

We knew they weren't far away; we could smell them and their droppings, aromatic as they cooked in the sun. We looked over the wall, and the contestants looked back at us with their mad, pale eyes, masticating slowly on some prerace treat, their chins fringed with wispy beards. They would have looked like dignified mandarins had it not been for the blue and white jockey caps that each of them was wearing, and their racing waistcoats, numbered to correspond with the list of runners. We were able to identify Bichou and Tisane and all the rest of them by name, but it was not enough to bet on. We needed inside information, or at least some help in assessing the speed and staying power of the runners. We asked the old man who was leaning on the wall next to us, confident in the knowledge that he, like every Frenchman, would be an expert.

"It's a matter of their *crottins*," he said. "The goats who make the most droppings before the race are likely to do well. An empty goat is faster than a full goat. *C'est logique.*" We studied form for a few minutes, and No. 6, Totoche, obliged us with a generous effort. "*Voilà*," said our tipster, "now you must examine the drivers. Look for a strong one."

Most of the drivers were refreshing themselves in the café. Like the goats, they were numbered and wore jockey caps, and we were able to pick out the driver of No. 6, a brawny, likely looking man who seemed to be pacing himself sensibly with the beer. He and the recently emptied Totoche had the makings of a winning team. We went to place our bet.

"*Non.*" Madame the bookmaker explained that we had to get first, second, and third in order to collect, which ruined our calculations. How could we know what the dropping rate had been while we were away looking at the drivers? A certainty had dwindled into a long shot, but we went for No. 6 to win, the only female driver in the race to come second, and a goat called Nénette, whose trim fetlocks indicated a certain fleetness of hoof, to come in third. Business done, we joined the sporting gentry in the little *place* outside the café.

The grand orchestra promised by the poster—a van from Apt with a sound system in the back—was broadcasting Sonny and Cher singing "I've Got You, Babe." A thin, high-chic Parisienne we recognized from the night before started to tap one dainty white-shod foot, and an unshaven man with a glass of *pastis* and a heavy paunch asked her to dance, swiveling his substantial hips as an inducement. The Parisienne gave him a look that could have turned butter rancid, and became suddenly interested in the contents of her Vuitton bag. Aretha Franklin took over from Sonny and Cher, and children played hopscotch among the goat droppings. The *place* was packed. We wedged ourselves be-

> France has found a unique way of controlling its unwanted critter population. They have done this by giving animals like snails, pigeons, and frogs fancy names, thus transforming common backyard pets into expensive delicacies. These are then served to gullible tourists, who will eat anything they can't pronounce; the French could serve *la waddle du gum à la sidewalk* and folks would still gobble it up.
>
> ◆
>
> —Chris Harris,
> *Don't Go Europe*

tween a German with a video camera and the man with the paunch to watch as the finishing line was prepared.

A rope was strung across the *place,* about eight feet above the ground. Large balloons, numbered from one to ten, were filled with water and tied at regular intervals along the length of the rope. Our neighbor with the paunch explained the rules: each of the drivers was to be issued a sharp stick, which had two functions. The first was to provide a measure of encouragement for any goats reluctant to run; the second was to burst their balloons at the end of the race to qualify as finishers. *Evidemment,* he said, the drivers would get soaked, which would be droll.

The drivers had now emerged from the café, and were swaggering through the crowd to collect their goats. Our favorite driver, No. 6, had his pocket knife out, and was putting a fine point on each end of his stick, which I took to be a good sign. One of the other drivers immediately lodged a complaint with the organizers, but the dispute was cut short by the arrival of a car which had somehow managed to creep down through one of the narrow streets. A young woman got out. She was holding a map. She looked extremely puzzled. She asked the way to the autoroute.

The way to the autoroute, unfortunately, was blocked by ten goats, two hundred spectators, and a musical van. Nevertheless, said the young women, that is where I am going. She got back into the car and started inching forward.

Consternation and uproar. The organizers and some of the drivers surrounded the car, banging on the roof, brandishing sticks, rescuing goats and children from certain death beneath the barely moving wheels. Spectators surged forward to see what was going on. The car, embedded in humanity, was forced to stop, and the young woman sat looking straight

ahead, tight-lipped with exasperation. *Reculez!* shouted the
organizers, pointing back in the direction the car had come
from, and waving at the crowd to make way. With a vicious
crunch of gears, the car reversed, whining angrily up the
street to the sound of applause.

The contestants were called to the starting line, and drivers
checked the fastening of the cords around the goats' necks.
The goats themselves were unaffected by the drama of the
occasion. No. 6 was trying to eat the waistcoat worn by No.
7. No. 9, our outsider, Nénette, insisted on facing backwards.
The driver picked her up by her horns and turned her
around, jamming her between his knees to keep her pointing in the right direction. Her jockey cap had been knocked
over one eye, giving her a rakish and demented air, and we
wondered about the wisdom of our bet. We were counting
on her to take third place, but with impaired vision and no
sense of geography this seemed unlikely.

They were under starter's orders. Weeks, maybe months,
of training had prepared them for this moment. Horn to
horn, waistcoat to waistcoat, they waited for the starting
signal. One of the drivers belched loudly, and they were off.

Within fifty yards, it became apparent that these goats
were not instinctive athletes, or else they had misunderstood
the purpose of the event. Two of them applied their brakes
firmly after a few yards, and had to be dragged along.
Another remembered what it should have done half an hour
before, and paused at the first bend to answer a call of nature.
Nénette, possibly because she was half-blinkered by her cap,
overshot the turn and pulled her driver into the crowd. The
other runners straggled up the hill, stimulated by various
methods of persuasion.

"Kick them up the arse!" shouted our friend with the

paunch. The Parisienne, who was hemmed in next to us, winced. This encouraged him to give her the benefit of his local knowledge. "Did you know," he said, "that the last one to finish gets eaten? Roasted on a spit. *C'est vrai.*" The Parisienne pulled her sunglasses from their nest in her hair and put them on. She didn't look well.

The course followed a circuit around the high part of the village, looping back down to the old fountain which had been transformed into a water obstacle with a plastic sheet stretched between some hay bales. This had to be waded or swum just before the final sprint to the line of balloons outside the café—a brutal test of coordination and stamina.

Progress reports were being shouted down by spectators at the halfway mark, and news reached us that No. 1 and No. 6 were fighting it out in the lead. Only nine goats had been counted going past; the tenth had *disparu*. "Probably having its throat cut," said the man with the paunch to the Parisienne. She made a determined effort, and pushed through the crowd to find less offensive company near the finishing line.

There was a splash from the fountain, and the sound of a woman's voice raised to scold. The water obstacle had claimed its first victim—a little girl who had miscalculated the depth, and who stood waist-deep in the water, bedraggled and bawling with surprise.

"*Elles viennent, les chèvres!*"

The girl's mother, in desperation at the thought of her child being trampled to a pulp by the contestants, hitched up her skirt and plunged into the water. "What thighs!" said the man with the paunch, kissing the tips of his fingers.

With a clatter of hoofs, the leading runners approached the fountain and skidded into the hay bales, showing very little enthusiasm for getting wet. Their drivers grunted and cursed and tugged and finally manhandled their goats into the water and out the other side to the finishing straight, their sodden espadrilles squelching on the tarmac, their sticks poised like lances. The positions at the halfway mark had been maintained, and it was still No. 1 and No. 6 Titine and Totoche, skittering up to the line of balloons.

No. 1, with an enormous backhand swipe, exploded his balloon first, showering the Parisienne, who stepped smartly backwards into a pile of droppings. No. 6, for all his stick sharpening before the race, had more difficulty, just managing to burst his balloon before the next runners reached the line. One by one, or in dripping groups, they staggered in until all that remained was a single swollen balloon hanging from the line. No. 9, the wayward Nénette, had not completed the course. "The butcher's got her," said the man with the paunch.

We saw her as we walked back to the car. She had broken her cord and escaped from her driver, and was perched high above the street in a tiny walled garden, her cap hanging from one horn, eating geraniums.

Peter Mayle spent fifteen years in advertising before turning to writing books. His work has been translated into seventeen languages, and he is best known for his books Toujours Provence *and* A Year in Provence, *from which this story was excerpted.*

*

The town was full of middle-aged English tourists having an off-season holiday (i.e., one they could afford). Wisps of conversation floated to me across the tables and from couples passing on the sidewalk. It was always the same. The wife would be in noise-making mode, that incessant, pointless, mildly fretful chatter that overtakes Englishwomen in mid-life. "I was going to get tights today and I forgot. I asked you to remind me, Gerald. These ones have a ladder in them from here to Amalfi. I suppose I can get tights here. I haven't a clue what size to ask for. I knew I should have packed an extra pair..." Gerald was never listening to any of this, of course, because he was secretly ogling a braless beauty leaning languorously against a lamppost and trading quips with some local yobbos on Vespas, and appeared to be aware of his wife only as a mild, chronic irritant on the fringe of his existence.

—Bill Bryson, *Neither Here Nor There: Travels in Europe*

* * *

Out of Teheran

On a cross-Asia bus journey, the passengers
learn the meaning of "no stoppage."

IT WAS ALREADY MIDAFTERNOON, BUT OUR FIRST STOP across the border was for breakfast. This wasn't surprising, since the trip from Teheran was already running ten hours behind schedule. Our first samples of leavened bread and baklava almost made us forget. So did a new crew of drivers who'd taken over the Mercedes-Benz bus. One of them, a stud who wore his shirt open to the belt buckle and flashed a smile full of gold-capped teeth, became their spokesman.

"Ladies and man, I am Kemil. All problems, come to me. We go now to Erzurum. No stoppage…. You see. Turk men good."

Yes, yes. At least, we had Rolf to entertain us. He'd been awake all night swapping yarns and insults with an American cowhand who'd been padding his savings account as a construction worker in Iran. They were a great pair because they'd yet to be spooked by any sight they'd seen. They compared notes on the one train across the Baluchi desert, which took three days and offered no food or water. There'd been plenty of rebels, however, who swooped in periodically on their camels and aimed machine-gun fire at the train.

"*Ach*. Dat is Asia." When Rolf said Asia, you realized the word had three syllables. "I vas dreaming the whole time of sauerbraten!"

"You go for that mangy stuff?" the American asked. "You must not be wrapped too tight."

"Ja. I am sick of rice and tea." It was a shocking admission. "Give me some fucking meat and potatoes. I say, I vant some fucking meat on ze plate!"

He was always playacting. This time, he spoke for some time to an imaginary waiter. He might have gone on for a hundred miles if the cowhand hadn't given him competition.

"Yeah, an' gimme a juicy rib-eye steak, butter-basted, with home fries and A1 sauce, an ice cream sundae and a few triple-thick slices of that Texas toast…"

"Nah, nah. German food it's best! I am sorry!"

"No, you ain't sorry!"

"Ja, ja. I am sorry. The German food ist best. *Schnitzel. Ach! Spaetzle. Ach!* Bring it over here, man, and hurry vith it!"

Across the aisle, a party of overweight Iranian Fuller Brush men was enchanted by another young American. They didn't know that he was a draft evader in permanent exile. All they knew was that he spoke perfect Farsi. Leaning forward in their seats, sweating in their rolled-up oxford shirts, they cooed appreciatively, called others on the bus to witness the spectacle and gazed at him as if he was the Messiah, or at least Zoroaster. It was some feat on the American's part to silence these gabby, expansive men. They'd been feeding the whole bus with slabs of bread, onslaughts of apricots and pistachios. Most of them were bald, but their faces were young, still straining fervently to meet the next new word, new sale, new insight. They made me feel like I was among my relatives at Passover. And why not? After all, the whole Middle East was Semitic, and so, it seemed, was I. In the salesmen's continual throwing out of arms, I recognized a familiar attempt to encircle the world, hug it close and thereby control it. I was at home with the giving, giving, giving that verged on bribery—wasn't that a little like what I'd been trying with my girlfriend Iris?

An hour or so after Kemil had promised "no stoppage," we did just that. There was no apparent reason for it, but the crew scattered before we could ask them for one. They abandoned us and the bus on the side of the road by the outskirts of a Turkish village just big enough to boast a mosque with a single minaret. This was one pit stop too many. Outside, the sun dipped toward Europe and heated the stilled bus. The Persians untucked their wrinkled shirts and snoozed. The rest of us wanted to get off, but to do so, we knew, would encourage the drivers to dally longer. It was enough to put Rolf in a fighting mood.

"Vat ze fuck ist with this death ship, eh? Ve start beating on our seats, ja? Dat's it…. Vun, two! Vun, two!" I followed his instructions.

John Krich is the author of several books including Why is This Country Dancing: A One-Man Samba to the Beat of Brazil, Won Ton Lust: Adventures in Search of the World's Best Chinese Restaurant *and* Music in Every Room: Around the World in a Bad Mood, *from which this story was excerpted.*

★

The teas and bread tasted amazingly good, as outdoor meals of crap can. We passed the tin can back and forth in silence, staring from the shadows of our greasy canvas kennel out at a bleak gray wilderness of stones and mud, as hot liquid thawed out aching muscles and numbed limbs. The weather boffins had come up with a new strain of snow, by the look of it. It fell in microscopic flakes like a mist of talcum powder, penetrating the skin's pores, then coating your bones with ice. When supplies ran out up there and a fresh batch had to be prepared, microsnow was replaced briefly by torrents of freezing slush. I found it impossible to imagine the desert being unbearably hot—or even warm.

"*Baard*," Nuri commented.

The word means "cold."

"*Fock*," he added, pointing up at Weather Control.

I agreed: "Fuck them. Quite right, Nuri. *Enough!*" I shouted at the churning charcoal fog. "Dump it on Riyadh! Give it to someone who needs it, you bastards!"

Nuri looked puzzled, scrutinizing the clouds to see who I was yelling at, then frowning at me. He'd probably said "*Foq*"—which means "above"—not "Fuck," I realized later.

—Paul William Roberts, *In Search of the Birth of Jesus:*
The Real Journey of the Magi

"Hey, Jack, which way to Mecca?"

Drawing by Peter Arno; © 1938 The New Yorker Magazine, Inc.

* ★ *

A Holy Holiday
in Hell

You don't have to be a religious zealot
to enjoy yourself in the Bible Belt,
but it certainly helps.

MY FRIEND DOROTHY AND I SPENT A WEEKEND AT HERITAGE USA, the born-again Christian resort and amusement park created by television evangelists Jim and Tammy Bakker, who have been so much in the news. Dorothy and I came to scoff—but went away converted.

Unfortunately, we were converted to Satanism. Now we're up half the night going to witch's Sabbaths and have to spend our free time reciting the Lord's Prayer backward and scouring the neighborhood for black dogs to sacrifice. Frankly, it's a nuisance, but if it keeps us from going to the Heritage USA part of heaven, it will be worth it.

Just kidding. In fact, we didn't actually come to Heritage USA to scoff. At least I didn't. I came because I was angry. Normally I take a live-and-let-live attitude toward refried Jesus-wheezing TV preachers. They've got their role in life, and I've got mine. Their role is to be sanctimonious panhandlers. My role is to have a good time. They don't pray for cocaine and orgies. I don't go on the tube and ask people to send me $100. But, when a place like Heritage USA starts advertising fun in the sun and Heritage's founders start having drug blasts and zany extramarital frolics, I feel they're stepping on my turf.

Heritage USA is a fair-size chunk of Christendom, 2,300 acres. It's half an hour from the go-go New South Sun Belt town of Charlotte, North Carolina—just over the border into the poky Old South Bible Belt county of York, South Carolina. The Heritage entrance gate appears to be a colonial Williamsburg turnpike toll plaza. Admission is free, however. Inside the gate you have the same vaguely depressing pine barrens that you have outside. A dozen roads meander through the scrub with the sly purposelessness of burglary lookouts.

Not that Heritage USA is an "empty vessel" (Jeremiah 51:34). By no means. Recreation facilities are "ministered unto you abundantly" (II Peter 1:11). There are playgrounds, kiddie rides, bridle paths, tennis courts and swimming pools, where I guess you have to lose faith at least temporarily or you'll just stand around on top of the water. And there are vacation cottages for rent and condo homes for sale, plus campgrounds and acres of gravel to park your Winnebago on. You can see the house where Billy Graham grew up and make *Amityville Horror* jokes about it. A golf course is being laid out. I'll rush back as soon as it's done, to hear what new kinds of blasphemy Christian golf leads to:

The rough ways shall be made smooth.—Luke 3:5

Thou shalt not lift up any iron.—Deuteronomy 7:5

This cup is the New Testament in my blood.

—I Corinthians 11:25

I will put my hook in thy nose. —II Kings 19:28

Midst these lesser marvels is an artificial lake with a fifty-two-foot water slide and the world's largest wave-making pool. A little choo-choo train goes all the way around the lake shore. And across from the train station is an enormous hotel, shopping mall, theater, restaurant and indoor inspirational loitering center.

The architects must have been touched by the holy spirit because they were definitely speaking the language of design in tongues when they did this. At one end there's the Heritage Grand Hotel—Georgian on steroids, Monticello mated with a Ramada Inn and finished in Wendy's Old Fashioned Hamburgers Gothic. This is attached to a two-hundred-yard stretch of bogus Victorian house fronts, which screen the shopping mall. The house fronts have extruded plastic gingerbread details and are painted in colors unfit for baboon posteriors. Interesting that the same God who inspired the cathedral at Chartres, Westminster Abbey and the Sistine Chapel also inspired this. That Big Guy Upstairs can be a real kidder.

The Christmas decorations were still up at Heritage. From the entrance gate all the way to the water slide, the place was festooned with yule lights and other pagan symbols of the season—tinseled evergreens, holly wreaths, snowmen, candy canes. But no Santa Claus. His elves were there, stuffing stockings and wrapping presents, but Santa himself was nowhere to be found. When we walked into the hotel lobby, carolers were singing:

> You'd better not frown,
> You'd better not cry,
> You'd better not pout,
> I'm telling you why.
> Jesus Christ is coming real soon.

And I thought Heritage USA was going to be dumb. But I'd only been there fifteen minutes and I was already confronted by enough serious theological questions to send St. Thomas Aquinas back to Bible college. Did Santa die on the cross? Will he be resurrected at Macy's? Were Christ's disciples really elves? When the second coming happens, will Jesus bring toy trains?

While I puzzled over these mysteries Dorothy went shopping. She's normally as good at this as any human female. But she was back in minutes with no bags or packages and a dazed, perplexed expression, like a starved Ethiopian given a piece of wax fruit. What could be the matter?

We went into the bookstore and I found out. There on the shelves were personal affirmations of faith by Roy Rogers and Dale Evans, a born-again diet plan, a transcription of the horrible (though rather unimaginative) things you can hear if you play rock and roll records backward, and a weighty tome arguing that every time the New Testament says "wine" it really means "grape juice." But I couldn't find anything you'd actually call a book. The Bibles themselves had names like *A Bible Even You Can Read* and *The Bible in English Just Like Jesus Talked*.

> ———— ☽ ————
>
> Cardinal O'Connor says all gay activists are going to Hell. So sometimes, when Harriet and I are sitting around wondering where to go on vacation, we think, well, Hell would be nice.
>
> ◆
>
> —Sara Cytron

Then we went into the music store. It was the same thing. There were racks of tapes and records by Christian pop groups, Christian folk groups,

Christian heavy-metal groups, Christian reggae groups, all of them singing original compositions about the Lord. No album was actually titled *I Found God and Lost My Talent,* but I'm sure that was just an oversight. There was even a "Christian Rap Music" cassette called *Bible Break:*

> The Bible is the holy book
> So let's open it up and take a look
> You got Genesis
> Exodus
> Leviticus
> Deuteronomy

And so on to Revelations with complete lack of rhythm or meter. (I was witnessing a miracle, I was sure, or auditing one anyway: here was something that sounded worse than genuine rap.)

The toy store was weirder yet. The stuffed toys had names like "Born-Again Bunny" and "Devotion Duck." A child-size panoply of biblical weapons was for sale, including a "shield of righteousness," a "helmet of faith," and a "sword of truth" that looked ideal for a "clobber of little sister." And there were biblical action figures—a Goliath with a bashed skull, David looking fruity in a goat-skin sarong, Samson and Delilah as Arnold Schwarzenegger and Maria Shriver. "Comes seductively dressed" read the sell copy on Delilah's bubble pack. Here was a shopper's hell indeed.

I looked at the people crowding the Heritage "Main Street" mall. They didn't seem to be having much fun. Many of them were old, none looked very well-off. There was a dullness in their movements and expressions. Even the little kids looked somber and thick. In the men's room stall where I went to sneak a cigarette there were only four bits of graffiti:

DO YOU KNOW WERE [SIC] YOU WIFE IS AT

JESUS IS #1

666

PLEASE DON'T MARK THESE WALLS

The last scratched into the paint with a key or pocketknife.

I almost don't have the heart to make fun of these folks. It's like hunting dairy cows with a high-powered rifle and scope. Then again, I have to consider what they'd do to me if they caught me having my idea of a vacation—undressed bimbo in a sleazy Florida hotel room, bottle of Vaseline Intensive Care lotion, some drugged wine…. In fact, you already know what they did when they caught Jim Bakker. Heck, they want to hang the likes of Jim and me. And all I want to do is rib them a little.

I've always figured that if God wanted us to go to church a lot He'd have given us bigger behinds to sit on and smaller heads to think with. But God or carbohydrates or something had done that for these people. They all had huge bottoms, immense bottoms. It looked like everyone in the place had stuffed a chair cushion down the back of his leisure slacks. And what leisure slacks! Heal them, oh Lord, for they are injured in the taste buds. Dorothy and I had dressed quietly for the occasion. But my button-down shirt and chinos and her blue blazer and tartan skirt made us stick out like nude calypso dancers. We were wearing the only natural fibers for 2,300 acres in any direction.

"You know what you've got here?" I said to Dorothy. "This is white trash behaving itself—the only thing in the world worse than white trash *not* behaving itself."

"Shhhhh!" said Dorothy. "That's mean."

"These people aren't having any fun," I said. "They should join the Klan. They'd be better off. They could hoot and holler and what-not. The Klan doesn't do all that much really bad stuff anymore because there are too many FBI double agents in it. And if these folks joined the Klan, they could smoke and drink again. Plus, they'd get to wear something halfway decent, like an all-cotton bed sheet."

"P.J.!" said Dorothy, "Stop it! Everybody can hear you."

"I'm serious," I said. "All you people, you really ought to..." Dorothy slapped a hand over my mouth and pulled me outside.

We took one more walk through the Heritage mall. I was eavesdropping hard, hoping for some final, telling quote. No luck.

Everybody was on good behavior just like the day before. There were no screaming toddlers, no running kids, no griping adults. It was like being in the First Church of Christ Hanging Out at the Mall. Dorothy heard a jewelry salesman tell his customer, "It has a lifetime guarantee—or until Jesus returns, whichever."

P. J. O'Rourke has written many books, including Parliament of Whores, All the Trouble in the World, Modern Manners, Republican Party Reptile, *and* Holidays in Hell, *from which this story was excerpted. Heritage USA closed its pearly gates for good in 1997, but it remains unlcear if it was P. J. O'Rourke's fault.*

※

I learned something the other day. I learned that Jehovah's Witnesses do not celebrate Halloween. I guess they don't like strangers going up to their door and annoying them.

—Bruce Clark

✦ ✶ ✦

The Duck of Peace

Crossing the border can ruin a guy's day.

"WHERE YOU FOLKS COMING FROM?" THE U.S. CUSTOMS agent asked, leaning down to give the inside of the van a quick once-over. His eyes widened.

"Mexico," Steve whispered, his hands gripping the steering wheel, eyes frozen on the inspection area ahead.

"What was that?" the agent said, bending closer.

"Mexico," Steve repeated, his eyes glassy, his breathing fast and shallow, complexion pasty beneath a heavy tan. The agent's attention moved from Steve's face to his hands, clenching and unclenching on the wheel.

"Are you all U.S. citizens?" he continued, glancing back at Lorena and then turning to me. His cheek twitched slightly as he noted my beard, my hair, my sandals. I felt like screaming, "Look at my J.C. Penney sport shirt and slacks! Can't you tell that I'm straight? This guy next to me is just naturally nervous; he's not a smuggler!"

"U.S. citizens?" Steve said, running his tongue over dry lips. Sweat beaded his forehead; it had been his idea to cross the border in late afternoon, in the heat of the day. "Day shift will be too hot and tired to tear us apart," he'd said, "and the evening shift won't be in high gear until later." I looked at the customs man. In spite of Steve's planning the officer looked as though they'd just lifted him off a coat hanger. The creases in his uniform were sharp enough to cut bread. Sweat began to pour down my chest.

"Yeah, we're U.S. citizens." Steve finally answered. He sounded about as convincing as if he'd claimed we were Russian ballerinas.

"How long have you been out of the United States?" the agent asked. The quickening excitement in his voice had been barely controlled: these weirdos were right out of a Customs Service training manual. He'd bet his badge against a six-pack of Lone Star that there was enough of *something*, somewhere inside this van, to get everyone on duty promoted on the spot. It would just be a matter of rooting it out.

When I went through customs as I was leaving Cuba, the customs person asked if I had anything to declare. "Yes," I announced, "I'm really glad I don't live here."

◆

—Anonymous

"Ah...well...a long time," Steve stammered, giving a sickly grin and shrugging his shoulders helplessly. The agent didn't bother to press for a more definite answer; without taking his eyes from us he backed into the booth and reached for the phone.

"Now you've really blown it!" I hissed. "I told you to let me drive through! He probably thinks we're the Mexican

Connection!" Steve waved his hands in front of his face; this was all too much for him, nothing was going according to The Plan. I stared out my window, grimly remembering all of our preparations, the long hours spent packing, cleaning and sorting. It had all gone to waste in a few moments, a few fumbled answers to simple questions. They'd tear us down to the frame and then chop up the pieces.

"Would you folks mind pulling up over there?" The agent's voice dripped with false sincerity as he pointed to a long metal table in the inspection area. Fluorescent lights cast an unforgiving glare on the shiny metal surface, banishing afternoon shadows. Behind the table stood a group of men and women in Customs uniforms. The staff had turned out to welcome us back.

"Yeah, sure," Steve croaked, lifting his foot off the clutch. He maneuvered the van alongside the waiting inspectors and stopped. He contorted his upper lip, chewing nervously on his moustache.

"Mind shutting it off?" a grey-haired man asked. Steve fumbled for the key. There was a long silence.

"Would you please step out now?" he added, giving the others significant looks. Steve opened his door and edged out cautiously. The older man smiled graciously; all he lacked was a long pointer: "Now, this, ladies and gentlemen, is your classic counter-culture smuggler. Please note the slight tremble at the knees and the furtive eye movements."

The agent waited for a few more moments and then said. "Now would you mind opening the doors of your vehicle so we can proceed?" One of the younger agents chuckled, but caught a quick look from the older man and turned it into a discreet cough. "Please take everything out," he added, a note of anticipation in his voice.

"*Everything?*" Steve asked, looking up hopelessly at the long roof rack, piled high with baskets, boxes and unidentifiable lumps and bundles.

"Everything!" the agent repeated, "Laid out on that table."

"Is this haaashish?" The agent drawled wearily, reaching into the hand-carved wooden chest. He gingerly removed a cylindrical bundle of heavy dark lumps wrapped in dried corn husks. After two hours, dreams of sudden promotion and banner headlines (*Trio Nabbed in World Record Haul of Zonko Root!*), had turned into a sweltering snipe hunt. The high good humor of the first hour, with many wisecracks about the incredible amount of junk we'd collected on our travels, was rapidly changing to a grim determination to find something, *anything* to justify the blitzkrieg search they'd dropped on us.

"No," I sighed. "That's not hashish. It's incense. Homemade *copal* incense from Chiapas." He gave me a doubtful look and managed a controlled, "We'll just check that out in the lab." While awaiting the results of the analysis, he pointed to the top of the van and said, "Get that box down, please."

I looked up. A vague premonition stirred in the back of my mind. Wasn't that box actually...?

"Hey, Steve!" I called. "They want to look at your box. You know, *the little one?*" Steve had been leaning against a tall steel stanchion, desperately trying to look casual. Whenever one of Lorena's plastic bags of herbs was sent off to the lab his knees buckled and his breathing became ragged.

At my mention of the box he took a few quick steps toward us and then stopped dead in his tracks, a look of complete panic twisting his face. He moved hesitantly to the van and began climbing slowly to the top, like a condemned man ascending a scaffold to perform the ultimate rope trick. As he handed the box down to me I caught the desperate message pulsing from his eyes; Think fast, smart ass, this was your idea!

I cradled the box in my arms and carried it to the table. The agent was busily burrowing through a huge pile of Mexican Indian clothing. "You folks have got enough stuff here to open your own store." He laughed, turning toward us with a weary smile. He looked at the box. The smile faded. "What in the...?" He stopped, eyes bulging slightly. His hand moved cautiously to the lid.

"Hahahaha! Well," I choked, "you see, it's a, it's a sort of a, you know...a...a coffin." Other inspectors, sensing the kill, quickly gathered around us, abandoning a detailed search of our dirty laundry, moldy tent and coffee cans filled with broken seashells.

"A coffin?" The question was a blend of outrage and disgust. "You mean that's a *baby coffin!*" he yelled, struggling to regain his composure. There were low growls from the assembled agents. How could I explain that it was actually a nicely crafted pine box that we'd bought from a Guatemalan carpenter? That with a bit of wood stain, varnish and some brass hinges we'd converted it into an ideal container for our odd and ends. It was a coffin only in name. It was a simple matter of *perspective*.

"Open!" he barked, sucking a great breath of air in anticipation of some unprecedented horror. His wife had been right, he should have gone into the Postal Service!

I twisted the little brass latch and raised the lid.

"Oh, Lord...!"

"You've gotta be...!"

"Unbelievable...!"

We stood in guilty silence, cries of outrage ringing ominously in our ears. Steve turned to face south, toward Mexico and freedom. I knew what he was thinking: Run! Now! While their attention was on the coffin…leap the pipe barricades…fast and low, crouching to avoid the .357 magnums…into that alley…shave his head…change identity…

The officer reached hesitantly into the coffin and began removing the little pink arms, torsos, legs and heads. His hands shook noticeably as he lined the grisly plastic parts along the edge of the inspection table. A miniature morgue.

"It's…it's kind of a long story!" I blurted, pulling my eyes away from the gruesome display. "You see we were camped on the Caribbean and every morning I went beachcombing…" They didn't seem to be listening; one of the older inspectors, a man who looked like my grandfather, was shaking his head from side to side. "I've seen it all now," his expression said; "It's time to retire!"

"….and I started noticing, you see, these, uh, pieces of doll babies all along the beach. An arm here, a head there. You know, litter. Doll baby litter. It seemed kind of, well, *hilarious*."

No one laughed.

"So then I started picking them up. Cleaning the beach, you might say." I hurried on, "And we had the coffin already, got it in Guatemala for a good price. Couldn't pass it up, actually. Seemed, well, *natural* to put the baby parts in it…"

At the word "natural" one of the women inspectors shuddered and steadied herself against the table. Others began drifting away, picking distractedly at the array of junk that had yet to be searched.

"I mean…don't you think it's…?" The agent raised his hand, cutting me off. I looked over at Steve and Lorena; they were staring at the corrugated metal roof.

A strategy conference convened. We stood nervously next

to the van, trying to ignore the occasional hard stare from the assembled inspectors. I had the feeling we were still a long way from an All American hamburger and cold beer. At least it was cooling off; the sun had gone down almost an hour before.

I quietly scooped up the pitiful remains of the doll babies and dumped them into the coffin, carefully closing the lid. Out of sight and out of mind, I hoped.

"Oh, boy, get ready," Steve muttered, watching as the meeting broke up, one officer going to the phone, another hurrying into the main building. They looked grim and determined. We had beaten the first wave, now they would call in the reserves.

The big black Labrador crouched in the back of the van, head tilted upward, his chest rising and falling as he howled mournfully. The handler turned to the chief inspector with a puzzled look. "I've never seen him do this before," he said, shaking his head in wonderment. The handler ordered the dog from the van, looking at us suspiciously.

"Whatever it is, it's weird!" he said, quickly leading the dog away. The agent glanced at his watch and then over at us. He'd thought of calling in sick, but had decided to come to work in spite of a nasty chest cold. Nights weren't so bad lately unless you got stuck with a bunch like this…

"He probably smelled the coyote," I offered. "We picked up this guy named Ramon, a rancher from around Monterrey. His pick-up had broken down and he had his pet coyote with him. Cute little thing, completely tame. He slept back there on the floor for a whole day."

The customs agent smiled knowingly. A clever story but not quite clever enough! He called to another man and ordered up a battery of powerful flood lights, a hydraulic jack, floor crawlers, stethoscopes, probes, hammers and whisk brooms.

"Or it could even have been the pig." Lorena added helpfully. "It took days just to clean up all of the…" Her voice trailed off; if he didn't believe the story of the coyote how would he handle a pregnant five-hundred-pound brood sow? "It was near Tepic," she continued. "Our landlord said he'd knock something off the rent if we'd take this pig to Guadalajara. His brother has a…"

The chief inspector turned his back on her, ending any further explanations.

"It's clean," an agent said half an hour later, pushing himself from beneath the van. No hidden compartments or clever modifications to hide illicit goods. Steve wiped sweat from his brow; he could take the same van through the border time after time and still worry that they'd manage to find something incriminating.

Another man was inside, tapping at the panelling with a tiny mallet. He worked as methodically and intently as a master safecracker, but found nothing. A third inspector scrutinized the screwheads attaching the panelling to the interior for scratches or other evidence that we had taken down the thin wood and stuffed the empty spaces with forbidden powders or herbs. Still others removed the headlights, hubcaps, heater ducts and heavy cardboard liners beneath the dashboard.

I was tempted to tell them that Steve's paranoia had driven us to check and clean those same spaces the day before. We had spent hours in the middle of the desert, sweating under a blazing sun, dusting, sweeping and washing every corner and crevice in the van. Two miles before the border crossing Steve had suddenly stopped, demanding that we swear an oath that we weren't smuggling anything. Lorena and I had answered with laughter, but Steve had insisted we pledge to be clean and innocent.

"A minute of paranoia is worth a year's detention!" he repeated, time after time, until I was ready to swear to anything just to get moving again.

Another conference was called, the inspectors moving carefully out of earshot. An argument seemed to have developed between those who had given up hope and those still thirsting for the kill. Fate intervened in the form of a brand new white Cadillac. The driver, a huge red-faced man wearing an improbably large cowboy hat, was having trouble understanding what was being asked of him.

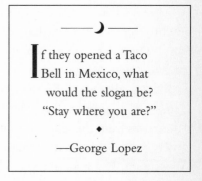

If they opened a Taco Bell in Mexico, what would the slogan be? "Stay where you are?"

♦

—George Lopez

"Open the trunk? What for? Some kind of trouble here?" He glared at us from around a thick cigar, as though we had brought this upon him. I looked at the various Customs people. Perhaps it was true; they all wore the expression of hungry frustrated sharks.

The man's wife, a small silver-haired woman, peered suspiciously through the tinted windows, looking at the inspectors as if they were bandits. One of them was standing behind the car, waiting for the trunk to be opened. The rear bumper seemed unusually low to the ground.

"Why don't you folks just pack your things up and go along your way?" the chief inspector said, his interest already focusing on the Cadillac. We sighed with relief; we'd be lucky to find a tavern open at this hour, but if we hurried...

"Don't forget your coffin!" one of them snarled.

"Well, that about does it!" Steve said, tying a final knot around the seabag and checking the lashings on the outboard motor. We squeezed into the front of the van, exhausted but triumphant: they hadn't found it! We still had it!

"ONE BOTTLE! ARE YOU SERIOUS?"

Steve had just put the van in gear. The man with the cowboy hat was waving his arms wildly, his face dark with anger. There were enough bottles of liquor on the inspection table to stock a large *cantina*.

"Check that out," Steve giggled, motioning toward the Cadillac. An inspector was helping the wife remove several large boxes from the rear seat. The sharks had found their prey.

We pulled by them slowly, chuckling with relief and amusement. The man in the cowboy hat glared malevolently, then suddenly leveled his smoking cigar at us like a pistol. "What in the hell do you call *that*?" he yelled.

Steve's head jerked forward. It was a classic trick, to turn attention to another when caught red-handed. I held my breath as Steve flicked on the headlights. If they were bright enough they might not…

"Hold it right there!" an inspector shouted, moving quickly in front of us. Steve stepped on the brake, then slumped over the wheel, nervously probing his teeth with a long thumbnail. I could imagine what he was thinking: "almost" only counts in horseshoes. They had us.

We got out of the van, joining the group of agents silently at the front bumper.

"OK, what is it?" the chief inspector asked, shining the beam of his flashlight onto the black fuzzy ball.

"It's a…" Steve hesitated. "It's a duck," he confessed, "The *Pato de Paz*."

"The Peace Duck?" someone sputtered.

I groaned. After the incident of the coffin, I would have thought they'd take a duck in stride.

"Well, you see…" he hesitated again; these people just didn't seem to have a sense of the bizarre humor that is so dear to Mexicans. But maybe, once they heard the story…"Carl had this terrific attack of diarrhea last year in Baja and…"

"You mean to say that this duck is from Baja California?" a stern voice interrupted, "and that you have had it in your possession for *more than a year?*"

"Well, yeah," Steve continued, "but like I said, Carl had this attack and wandered off into the bushes and found the duck. In a bush. It was dead, you see, but it had got hung up in this bush. Perfectly dried out. Preserved, just like a mummy."

Heads nodded. Mummy, doll baby parts. Coffin. Oh, yes.

Steve hurried on with the story. "You see it occurred to us that it would be neat to wire him to the front bumper, like a hood ornament or a mascot. Mexicans loved it. Every time we stopped it drew a crowd. Nobody has ever tried to steal it. We don't even have to take it in at night."

Heads nodded again. Yes they could certainly understand why we didn't have to take it in at night. Steve began to elaborate on the tale, but the words weren't coming out quite right. He choked, stammered and then suddenly buckled forward. He jammed a fist into his mouth as great bellows of laughter reverberated off the metal ceiling overhead. Several hours of tense waiting had taken their toll on our sanities; Lorena and I joined him, tears streaming down our faces. The Customs agent grew more and more impassive.

As our fits passed one of the inspectors stepped forward and between tightly clenched jaws said: "Under the Endangered Species Act...of...1973...I hereby...confiscate...*this duck!*"

His self control suddenly slipped. Before we could protest he reached down, grabbed the Peace Duck and jerked it toward him.

Steve looked sadly at the empty bumper. The duck had seen a good many miles, from northern Baja to El Salvador and back, through deserts, jungles, mountains and cities, spreading peace and good will to millions. Well, hundreds at least. He reached down and gently pried the skinny little legs from the piece of twisted coathanger. After carefully brushing the brittle black feet against his shirt to clean off the dust and road grime, Steve handed them solemnly to the seething customs man. "Don't forget his feet; they're endangered, too."

As we climbed back into the van, the inspectors were walking slowly back toward the Cadillac. Their shoulders were slumped, their pace weary. It had been such a long day.

Carl Franz is the author of the much-acclaimed and repeatedly-reprinted The People's Guide to Mexico.

*

I had brought with me a yellow backpack so enormous that when I went through customs I half expected to be asked, "Anything to declare? Cigarettes? Alcohol? Dead horse?"

—Bill Bryson, *Neither Here Nor There: Travels in Europe*

DAVE BARRY

⋆ ⋆ ⋆

It's Monday...So This Must Be My Tax Write-Off in London

*The author finds speaking English is
not all it's scumbled up to be.*

RECENTLY, MY SON AND I SPENT A WEEK IN LONDON, WHICH is a popular foreign place to visit because they have learned to speak some English over there. Although frankly they have a long way to go. Often, when they get to the crucial part of a sentence, they'll realize that they don't know the correct words, so they'll just make some silly ones up. I had a lot of conversations that sounded like this:

ME: Excuse me. Could you tell us how to get to Buckingham Palace?

BRITISH PERSON: Right. You go down this street here, then you nip up the weckershams.

ME: We should nip up the weckershams?

BRITISH PERSON: Right. Then you take your first left, then you just pop 'round the gorn-and-scumbles, and, Jack's a doughnut, there you are!

ME: Jack's a *doughnut*?

BRITISH PERSON: Right.

Also they have a lot of trouble with pronunciation, because they can't move their jaw muscles, because of malnutrition caused by wisely refusing to eat English food, much of which was designed and manufactured in medieval times during the reign of King Walter the Mildly Disturbed. Remember when you were in junior high school, and sometimes the cafeteria workers would open up a large Army-surplus food can left over from the Spanish-American War and serve you a scary-looking dish with a name like "Tuna Bean Prune Cabbage Omelet Casserole Surprise"?

Well, they still have a *lot* of food like that over in England, on permanent display in bars, called "pubs," where people drink for hours but nobody ever eats. We saw individual servings of pub food that we recognized from our last visit, in 1978. Some dishes—no effort is made to conceal this fact—contain *kidneys*. We also saw one dish with a sign next to it that said—I swear I am not making this up—"Spotted Dick."

The English are very good at thinking up silly names. Here are some actual stations on the London underground: Marylebone, Tooting Broadway, Piccadilly Circus, Cockfosters, Frognal, Goodge Street, Mudchute, Barking and East Ham. Londoners are apologetic about their underground, which they believe has become filthy and noisy and dangerous, but which is in fact far more civilized than the average American wedding reception. At the height of rush hour, people on the London underground actually say "excuse me." Imagine what would happen if you tried an insane stunt like that on the New York City subway. The other passengers would take it as a sign of weakness, and there'd be a fight over who got to keep your ears as a trophy.

Our primary cultural activity in London was changing money. We had to do this a lot because the dollar is very weak. Europeans use the dollar primarily to apply shoe polish. So every day we'd go to one of the money-changing places that are all over London, and we'd exchange some dollars for British money, which consists of the "pound" and a wide variety of mutant coins whose sizes and shapes are unrelated to their values, and then we'd look for something to eat that had been invented in this country, such as pizza, and we'd buy three slices for what we later realized was $247.50, and then we'd change some money again. Meanwhile the Japanese tourists were exchanging *their* money for items such as Westminster Abbey.

> **E**uropean subways will give you a bit of culture shock the first time you ride them because you will probably not get mugged.
>
> ◆
>
> —Chris Harris,
> *Don't Go Europe*

In the interest of broadening my ten-year-old son's cultural awareness, we visited some important historic sites, including the Tower of London, the London Dungeon, and Madame Tussaud's Wax Museum, all of which are devoted to explaining in clinical detail how various historic members of royalty were whacked into small historic pieces. English history consists largely of royal people getting their heads chopped off, which is why members of the royal family now wear protective steel neck inserts, which is why they walk the way they do.

Needless to say, this brand of history was a hit with my son. He especially enjoyed the guided "Jack the Ripper" tour that we took one dark night with a very intense guide. "Right on this spot is where they found the victim's intestines," she'd say. "And right here is where they found the liver, which is now part of the food display of that pub over there."

Another cultural activity we frequently engaged in was looking the wrong way before attempting to cross streets. The problem is that in America, people drive on the *right* side of the street, whereas in London, they drive on *both* sides of the street, using hard-to-see cars about the size of toaster ovens. The best way to handle this, as a tourist, is to remain on one side of the street for your entire visit, and see the other side on another trip.

But I definitely recommend London for anybody who enjoys culture and could stand to lose a few pounds. I learned many things that will be of great value to me, not just personally, but also professionally, and I'm not saying that just to be polite to the English. I'm saying it because of Internal Revenue Service regulations.

Dave Barry also contributed "Failing to Learn Japanese in Only Five Minutes" to this book. He is regarded as one of the funniest writers in America by several people besides his publicist.

*

In an effort to boost orange juice sales in predominantly continental breakfast-eating England, a campaign was devised to extol the drink's eye-opening, pick-me-up qualities. Hence, the slogan, "Orange juice. It gets your pecker up."

—Marketing Boo-boos

DAVID ARIZMENDI

* * *

Of Generals and Gentlemen

A man's greatness is hard to measure.

IN ITALY, EVERYTHING IS SHROUDED BY THE HAZE OF Byronic glory. A puddle in the street is no puddle; it's an urban lagoon that makes you want to give it a coin and wish for something big. An alley is not a narrow passageway between buildings, but a shadowy tunnel whose versatility permits it to be the ideal backdrop for an ardent lovers' reunion, an out-of-body religious rebirth, or a covert exchange between two secret agents.

Imagine, if you will, the Isle of Capri on a late October afternoon. It's an hour or so by ferry from Sorrento. Physically, it's separated from the mainland only by a couple of miles. But if we view the mainland in its broader context as home to all that is earthly and mundane, Capri is light years away. Jason, my travel companion, and I sensed this on the boat. I remember we applauded—searching awkwardly for a way to express our awe—as we approached the high cliffs and sun-baked houses of the island, and a pleasant lady thanked us in broken English. This sparked a conversation between us, which continued until we said something in our miserable Italian which must have been terribly offensive, for she abruptly walked off the boat and disappeared into the crowd.

Jason was hungry; it had been over two hours since lunch. Eating six meals a day was my response to a seemingly endless bounty of delicious food that was too constricted by the breakfast-lunch-dinner routine. At first, our stomachs were a little challenged. Three weeks into our trip, however, we had developed a food dependency so severe that as soon as the satiated sensation that follows a big meal subsided, we were like prisoners in some deep dungeon, salivating over the dream of another meal. We needed to find somewhere to eat.

In Italy, this is not a difficult mission, and a few turns along a principal cobbled causeway brought us to an appealing *trattoria*. Warm, scarlet curtains framed tiny windows and the dim light that escaped reminded me of laughing eyes behind a veil. The roof was low and the walls were yellowed with the melancholic wisdom that accompanies the older buildings in Italy's countryside. This vision of delicacy and the seductive aroma of garlic and cheese caused us to hasten our step, but we abruptly halted when we noticed the man racing us to the door.

Immediately, we knew we were, on this little street in Capri that obscure October afternoon, experiencing that rare intimacy with greatness that comes once in a lifetime. As the man who helped Lincoln out of his carriage or the boy who shined Churchill's shoes would spend the rest of their lives talking about it, we knew this was The Moment, not only of our Italy trip, but—quite possibly—of our mortal existence.

His greatness was ineffably projected by his appearance. He was tall, and positioned at a forward angle so that his chin

protruded several inches beyond the rest of his facade. White
hair neatly peered out from under a tight, blue cap to border
his face, a chiseled, weathered, and, like some battleship that
emerges triumphant from a fierce naval battle, gloriously
defiant masterpiece. His gait was regulated but intense, like a
soldier under fire, and I was almost nonplussed when I noticed, as a final detail, his blue jacket completely laden with
an array of medals that caught the afternoon sun and seemed
to cascade like a shower of celebrating gunfire around him.
Here was a man!

Here was a man who undoubtedly conquered Ethiopia!
Here was a man who certainly knew Mussolini! Here was
one of the last warriors worthy of comparison with
Alexander and Charlemagne! And as he grabbed the door
handle and glanced at us over his shoulder, as if he was re-
viewing his troops one final time before leading them into
battle, I felt like dropping to my knees and begging to kiss
the hem of his military garb.

And then: *"Prego."* With a gracious smile and a subtle nod,
he swung the door open and shuffled to the side, making
way. He, the great gentleman, was basking in his benevolence
and waiting for the two foolish Americans from lower-
middle-class neighborhoods to enter before him.

Jason, nervously, stepped forward, but I snatched at his arm.
Was he mad? I panicked. This show of goodwill was certainly
perfunctory, but little more. It is for the mighty to offer; it is
for the meek to decline. For us to precede his entry would be
like two water-boys beating Washington across the Delaware.
It would be a violation of The Way Things Are, and would
reveal our naïve ignorance far more vehemently than the
guide book hanging out of my pocket or the Lifesavers on
my breath. Il Generalissimo would not be let down by us.

So, I deftly swept up to the door, reaching behind the General and opening it even farther. He spun around, surprised at my uncannily appropriate response, and stared at me forcefully as I beamed, "Oh, no. *Prego, signor.*" The Italian at work.

I suppose his experience with Americans had been limited to treaty conferences, for his astonishment at my respect was strong enough that he—as if, perhaps, refusing to believe all of the anti-American stereotypes were false—offered again. "*Prego,*" he announced, more carefully, as if he said it too sloppily the first time

I would have none of it, however. Caesar refused the crown thrice, remember. I pulled the door open farther, so that it was now completely out of contact with the General, giving me the upper hand. There would be no surrender. "*Signor, prego,*" I ventured with enough force to have Jason, from behind, groan an emphatic grunt of agreement.

The General suddenly looked upset. Perhaps, I wondered, he had won all of his medals fighting against the Americans and this display of international grace was too hard to stomach. Should we back down? No, I decided, his nervousness made the need for the proper respect even more apparent. When the General turned toward the restaurant and pointed at the interior angrily, I held my ground.

"*Prego!*" I was a little too loud, thinking volume would resolve the crisis.

The General yelled right back, "*Prego! Prego!*" He then exploded into a fit of Italian that frightened us with the harshness of its timbre and the tension of its tone, gesticulating wildly at the restaurant and then at us. It made Jason step back a bit, and I had practically decided to just run into the building when a mustached man—obviously alarmed by the several ancient curses being heaped upon our families by the

General—ran out. He surveyed the situation immediately and, putting a reassuring hand on the arm of the gentleman, asked, "What is the problem here?"

I was too shocked that he knew we were American to respond, but Jason answered, "We were just waiting for the officer to enter."

"Officer?" he asked.

"Yes, a decorated member of the armed services," I clarified, inexplicably happy that his English was imperfect.

"He is no officer! This man is our doorman!"

Those words fell upon us with the weighty strength of a murder verdict. It suddenly all made sense and we realized how stupid we were and the two of us just limply stood there. The only other time I had felt so devastatingly vulnerable was when the girl I had taken out for my first date told me, at the end of the evening, that my fly was open. But this was worse…this involved the whole scheme of Civilization.

The restaurant manager explained in rushed Italian to the doorman what had happened, and he laughed nearly as heartily as the restaurant staff did shortly after, and as the customers—one table at a time—did for the next few hours after that. Free drinks were showered upon our table by appreciative new friends and the manager kept us there all through the evening, forcing us to amass a plethora of acquaintances of which no mere tourist could boast.

And so, in the upside-down, wonderful confusion that traveling inspires, our respect toward the General did initiate us into the massive spiritual panorama that is Italy.

David Arizmendi submitted this story for the Travelers' Tales Italy Writing Contest.

At a Paris restaurant where diners share tables, I came that close to pouring a tablemate's wine over my salad. I thought it was a cruet of vinegar.

The lady was very nice. When I realized my mistake (divine intervention, I think) I returned the carafe to its place by her plate, mumbling my excuse. She merely smiled and said, "I was wondering…"

This woman probably still remembers me and my girlfriend—if not for my salad faux pas, then because my friend put on quite a display of groveling for a cigarette from our surly waiter. She even grabbed his apron. I think she might have kissed it. The tobacco shops had closed before she could restock and she had already gone a long time, for her, without a smoke.

The waiter was amused and gave her a cigarette. As she brought it to her mouth, trembling, her eyes met our tablemates'.

"Do you mind?" she asked, a puppy-dog look on her face.

"How could we, now?" said the same tolerant woman.

> —Sophia Dembling, "To Err is Humorous,"
> *The Dallas Morning News*

JON CARROLL

* ✳ *

The Great Invisible Pheasant Hunt

It's the manly thing to do.

WE WERE STAYING IN A CRUMBLING PALACE IN THE TOWN OF M—, in the arid western region of India called Rajasthan. We were guests of the maharajah's son and his wife.

We had arrived there, rogue journalists on a tour of odd backwaters, because there was some thought that the maharajah's son might turn the palace into a hotel. He was, quite frankly, strapped for cash—not like the glorious past, when hereditary feudal rulers could levy taxes whenever they felt like it. Those were the bad old days, unless you happened to be a maharajah.

The maharajah's son and his wife were about the same age as my wife and I. We were all four of us talkative; we were all curious. He poured whiskey after whiskey; we talked and we talked. Dinner receded infinitely. At around 9:30, we began dropping hints, but it was not until midnight that we actually sat down to solid food.

During the course of this marathon chat session, the maharajah's son asked me if I wanted to go pheasant hunting the next day.

"Of course," I said boisterously. I had never hunted a pheasant, or indeed anything at all, in my life.

"Wonderful!" he said. "I shall await you at 6:30!" I believe we toasted each other at that point. It was a jolly moment of cross-cultural camaraderie.

The next morning was not quite so jolly. I was up and dressed and bright-eyed and nauseated at 6:30; I sat in the big room ("living" room? I have no idea) and waited for my host to arrive. I pictured him in jodhpurs—we were not that far from the actual city of Jodhpur.

But there was only silence in the great palace. Not a creature was stirring, not even a scion.

I went ambling down the empty halls. "Hello?" I called. "Hello?" There was only silence. I came upon courtyards that I had not noticed before; I surprised elderly women beating wet clothing with rocks.

"Hello," I said. They drew back in horror.

I wanted more than anything to go back to bed. I wanted more than anything to take this deep silence throughout the palace as a sign. I wanted to delay as long as possible the actual hunting of the pheasant.

My experience with guns was limited to a .22 (target practice as a youth, for increased manliness) and an M-1 (ROTC as a youth, to increase our nation's readiness to meet aggression). The idea of taking whatever weapon was handed me and blasting away at a rapid and blameless bird…what could I have been thinking?

But I did not wish to disgrace myself. I did not wish to let our side down. Perhaps he meant to meet me at the front portico, or at the garage, or in yet another courtyard. So I wandered, head pounding, fear clutching at my gut. "Hello?"

Finally came the answering call. I stood stock still. It came again. I answered. After a minute, the maharajah's son appeared at the head of the staircase. He was in sleeping attire. His hair was mussed. He was scratching his head.

"I thought of the hunting to the pheasant we were have been going to go an hour ago," I remarked, inventing a new tense, the past perfect humiliative.

"Right you are," he said. "Right you are." Still he stood there. "Right you are. I'll just…"

"By all means," I said. "I'm fine."

He went away and I went back to the big room. I sat in an overstuffed chair and read one of those British magazines featuring stout women holding stout chrysanthemums. Time passed slowly. I began dreaming of antacid tablets.

He appeared at the door, dressed and vigorous. "Right then. Early start. Best thing. Shotgun all right?"

"Shotgun would be splendid," I said. We were both lying through our teeth.

So I was experiencing serious breakfast deprivation, and my head hurt just a little, and the Jeep was bouncing along a severely rutted road, and there was a shotgun with my name on it somewhere in the back.

Next to me was the maharajah's son. We were in Rajasthan, a part of India that looks a lot like Palmdale.

> A lot of qualifications to sit next to that exit door, huh? When did that happen? I've been a physical klutz for years. I'm like Clouseau. Nobody's ever said a word. All of a sudden they want me to be a fucking Navy SEAL.
>
> ◆
>
> —Dennis Miller, *The Rants*

Some of Rajasthan has the stark, desolate beauty of the great deserts of the world, but we were not in that part.

We were in the scrubby, bumpy, dotted-with-stunted-trees, already-too-hot-at-nine-in-the-morning part. We were off to shoot some pheasant. It was not something that either of us wanted to be doing, but we were doing it anyway. Such is the grave courtesy of our two great nations!

We reached a spot where someone had once seen a pheasant. The maharajah's son and I got out of the Jeep. He handed me the shotgun. It was the first shotgun I had ever held. Fortunately, I am an American; I knew how to hold it without looking stupid.

I was going to be fine, I knew, until it came time to fire it. But after that… began obsessing about the "kick." I knew that average citizens were always surprised by how much recoil a weapon has. "It's not like in the movies," they would stereotypically remark, while being treated for a dislocated shoulder.

"Fine day for a hunt," said the maharajah's son.

"Fine, fine day," I said. My mouth twisted upward.

Some men were sent out to belabor the bushes. They were the "beaters" (I knew this from mystery stories); their job was to flush a startled pheasant from its lair. Then we would merrily blast away at the damn thing. That was the plan.

The men disappeared over the lumpy horizon. We could hear their patented pheasant-frightening calls. "Woo-eee," came the ghostly cries. "Woo-eee."

We stood there with our weapons. A bead of sweat ran down my cheek. We stood there and stood there. The choir invisible continued to frighten putative pheasants in the distance.

Finally, the men reappeared. One waved his hands and shouted in a foreign tongue. "Good, they've got one," said the maharajah's son. We peered into the scrub before us. It was silent and still; not a leaf moved.

"There it is!" he yelled.

I peered more deeply into the underbrush. I saw nothing. "Where?" I asked.

The maharajah's son pointed. "Just by that big yellow rock. You can see the feathers." Still, I saw nothing.

"Oh, yes," I said confidently.

"Your shot, then. Quickly now." Swell. I put the shotgun to my shoulder. I wondered about the state of orthopedic surgery in rural India. I fired in the direction of the yellow rock.

"Splendid. You've winged him." He called out to the beaters. They loped purposively off down a gully. "Fine shot," said my host.

"And the gun didn't really hurt my shoulder," I said. He looked at me curiously. Probably that's not a sentiment that pheasant hunters share with each other.

The beaters returned fifteen minutes later. They could not locate the wounded pheasant. "Bad luck," said the maharajah's son.

"Perhaps you'll score a clean kill," I suggested. I was swaggering just a bit—wounded bird, intact shoulder, manly chat with demi-royalty.

"I think not," said the maharajah's son. "Hot day today. I'd enjoy a whole day of sport, but duty calls. Duty calls."

It was the graceful way out. An expedition desired by no one had concluded with the imaginary wounding of an invisible bird. We had successfully agreed to tell the same lie, which is the essence of courtesy.

Jon Carroll writes a daily column for the San Francisco Chronicle.

*

I was number 6 on the waiting list for a morning flight from New Delhi to Agra. The aircraft had a capacity of about one hundred or so. When the agent came to the small desk to begin the process of determining who was there and who would be given a seat, a crowd of at least two hundred surged forward, carrying me along with it. Suddenly I was aware that I was virtually carrying someone piggy-back. I turned around as best I could and confronted a man who had casually started to climb over me. I asked him what the hell he was doing, and he responded that he was on the waiting list.

"So am I," I said, "but I'm not climbing over the other passengers. Why don't you take it easy?"

"I cannot," he replied. "I am number 83 on the waiting list."

—Robert J. Matthews, "Keep 'em Flying!"

DAVID LEAVITT

* * *

Cena

*For some reason, speaking a foreign
language makes it easier to fit
your foot in your mouth.*

THE FIRST TIME I CAME TO ITALY ALONE, I LACKED THE
knack for meeting strangers. Once in Bologna, out of desperation, I tried to have a chat with the stout *padrona* of my
pension, who happened to own a little Pekingese dog.
Although I could speak only two sentences in Italian—*"per
favore, parla inglese?"* and *"per favore, parla francese?"*—I thought
to myself, the word for dog in French is *chien*; and since
Italian words are basically French words with an "a" on the
end, I pointed to the animal and said, *"cena?"* at which point
the woman's eyes bulged in horror as she grabbed the beast
protectively to her breast.

As I learned later, *cena* means dinner.

This was by no means the last of the mistakes I made in
Italian; in fact, ten years later, when I'd actually studied and
begun to learn the language, I started making even more.
Once in Sestri Levante, for instance, my friend Giovanna and
her very correct Milanese parents and I were talking about
the various resort towns near Genova, one of which is called

Chiavari. *"Ti piace Chiavari?"* I asked Giovanna's mother, who went white. Later, Giovanna explained to me that by mispronouncing *"Chiavari"* as *"chiavare,"* I had asked her mother if she liked to fuck.

Mistakes go in the other direction, too. A charming example of awkward translation is the English menu we were handed at one of those places one goes to once. In this case the imaginative author, knowing that *primi piatti* means "first courses" and *secondi piatti* "second courses," sensibly rendered antipasti as *"course d'oeuvres."*

Finally this: Italians (like Spaniards) have great difficulty hearing the difference between certain English words: "chip" and "cheap" sound almost identical to their ears; so, too, "pip" and "peep," or "dip" and "deep." Thus you can imagine the surprise of an Italian friend when he went to an American supermarket and found a toilet paper roll that proclaimed "1000 SHEETS."

"America is a wonderful country," he said.

David Leavitt is the author of Family Dancing, The Lost Language of Cranes, *and* While England Sleeps. *He is also the co-author, with Mark Mitchell of* Italian Pleasures, *from which this story was excerpted.*

*

Chicken-man Frank Perdue's slogan, "It takes a hard man to make a tender chicken," got terribly mangled in Spanish translation. A photo of Perdue with one of his birds appeared on billboards all over Mexico with a caption that explained, "It takes a hard man to make a chicken aroused."

—Marketing Boo-boos

SUSAN STORM

. * .

An Alarming Time

*Think thrice before requesting a
wake-up call in India.*

WHEN I WAKE IN MY OWN BED, I RELY ON THE RADIO, THE
neighbor's lawnmower, or my body clock to tell me when
the day has to start. But when I travel, I give this massive
responsibility to someone who goes to work on a camel,
faces east when he sleeps, and possibly has boiled goldfish for
breakfast. And I'm always surprised when things go wrong.

The venue and characters may change from city to city,
but the debacle always sorely tests my resilience. This time
I'm in Delhi, a spectacular city of silver and saffron, dancing
bears and wailing *muezzins*. I request a 4 a.m. wake-up call
and a car to take me to the airport. Then I settle down to
what I think will be a good eight hours sleep.

I dream of elephants with painted tusks, of narrow streets and
brass urns that gleam in dark corners, of seduction by sultry
princes, and of being deafened by clanging musical instruments.

The room is reverberating with the noise of a thousand
organ-grinding monkeys. I open one eye, it's midnight. The
telephone. "Hello," I mumble.

"Susan Storm? Is okay we be waking you at four?"

I grunt acknowledgement and struggle back to sleep through the noise of a thudding generator and blaring traffic. The phone rings so loud, again, that I wake with my heart beating like a distant drum in my mouth. It's one-forty-five.

"Hello. Mr. Surinder? Here is time to *wake up!*" I lie for several minutes with the receiver in my hand, as if I've been stabbed. The precious hours are leaking away. I pop a Valium.

I dream I'm in Bosnia. There is an explosion of sound again, close to my head. I lift the receiver without thinking, programmed as I am to answer to technology. Two-thirty. "*Wake up! wake up!* Mrs. Sting! *Wake up!*"

My voice is cold as ice. "Four. I said *four* o'clock." Then I wonder what the penalty is for death by insult in this country of an eye for an eye. I stare at the ceiling, listening to my clanging heart, the cacophony of wedding celebrations emitting from the ballroom below, and firecrackers exploding in the dense night sky.

Three-fifteen. "Miss Form? You wanting breakfast when you be waking at four?" I threaten with arson, with vivisection, with circumcision. I try a last, frantic effort to silence the machinations that are tearing my nerves to pieces. I tell the voice I will write nasty things about his hotel. There's a timid knock on my door a few minutes later. The turbaned telephonist has brought me a cup of fragrant tea with a wedge of muslin-wrapped lemon. "Help you be sleeping!" he exclaims, his slash of teeth like a new moon on a dark night.

I stare at the heavy black instrument of torture willing it not to ring. It hypnotizes me into a sleep as deep as if I have been lobotomized.

The phone shrieks. I leap out of bed as if it has been

booby-trapped, and fall over my packed cases. Dawn is creeping under the curtains. It's five-thirty.

"Dr. Stream? This is Mufta from the lobby. You is supposed to be here long time since. Your car she is waiting late."

I glower at the Indian skyline where the sun is a molten blob crawling over the thickly-polluted sky.

Struggling with my luggage, I step in a plate of food outside my door. The smells of moghul chicken and yoghurt, saffron rice, and mint hit my nostrils. The morning paper on the mat shouts of the injustices of the night and I tend to agree.

I tear like a banshee through the doors, and the doorman shouts after me as I slide down the marble steps.

"You sleep good? Miz Strong?"

On the way to the airport we pass a man washing in the fountains, a white cow, and an elephant with sequins glued to its cracked back ambling home after a night in the grounds of a grand hotel. A bear wearing a torn tutu and a studded collar limps alongside a young boy, and a turbaned, bearded Sikh and his four children on a motor scooter negotiates the morning traffic.

We hurtle past tiny shops that sell corks, exotic essences, and silk of every hue, tassels, brocades, and tin buckets, sacks of garlic, ropes of necklaces, skeins of jute, carved wooden horses, *chapatti* boxes, and sweet smelling garlands of jasmine.

I ask the taxi driver to stop. The young girl wants a crazy price for the garlands, but I buy three. I place one each around hers and the driver's necks, and he hangs one around mine.

The plane is delayed as I suspected it would be, but I'm not annoyed. I smell my jasmine garland and finger it like a talisman and realize India's ineptitudes are the flaws in an ancient glittering tapestry. The littered streets become magic carpets, the greasy tea a potion, the Sikh a wizard, the flickering lights a genie's lamp, the opaque windows a crystal ball. India has me under her spell, and I'm hypnotized into staying.

To hell with the alarm clock.

Susan Storm is a widely published photojournalist working for Australian and international magazines and newspapers. Born in Prague, she grew up in South Africa, and is still growing up in Australia.

*

I went to the airport. I had three pieces of luggage. I said that I want this piece to go to Cleveland, this piece to Toronto, and this piece to Florida. The airline agent said, "We can't do that." I replied, "Well, you did it last week."

—Henny Youngman

PAUL WILLIAM ROBERTS

* * *

This Land is Mine

No it's not!

NURI HAD FOLLOWED A CURIOUSLY ERRATIC ROUTE, ZIG-
zagging for no apparent reason. But since my camel—now
named Mustafa—seemed incapable of doing anything but
follow Nuri's confident mount, I had little choice but to trail
behind. No doubt I'd bought a lemon, but at least it
worked—it even ran, but only when Nuri's camel broke
into the occasional canter itself.

I dismounted, tying Mustafa to a rock—as Nuri had done
with his beast—and attempted to protest this unexpected
halt. Nuri was far from stupid, but he was also far from rocket
science. In the old days, perhaps, he would have been termed
a "simpleton." It wasn't possible to argue with him, I realized,
because he only did what was currently programmed into
him, and I had not written the program. As I reluctantly
unhooked my knapsack and stuff pack from Mustafa's tattered saddle, Nuri gestured around himself at the bleak,
crepuscular wilderness, saying,

"Land-iss mine…"

"Yes," I replied, marveling at the Bedouin feeling for territory, at their innate sense of where they belonged and what belonged to them. "Yes. *Your* land…"

"Land-iss *mine*," he said, more forcefully, sweeping his arm in an arc at all ahead.

"Yes, yes. The great Bedouin desert. Where your people have lived for *thousands* of years."

He seemed angry now, repeating the gesture and the phrase. *"Land-iss mine!"*

Oh Christ! I thought. He's going loony on me. I started to clear an area of small rocks and stones, where I planned to attempt sleep, when I discovered, after scooping away some gravel, a round black cylinder of metal. About to call Nuri and ask him to take a look, it suddenly struck me that his proprietorial announcement was nothing of the sort.

"Right," I said. "Here's one, Nuri! Isn't this a land mine?"

He plodded over and peered down, lighting a match.

"Ah! Land-iss mine," he agreed happily.

No wonder we'd been zigzagging.

I could have had it as a pillow—for a second. Always trust a Bedouin, particularly when you have no choice but to trust one. An old British diplomat once confided this useful piece of information to me. It's worth remembering.

Paul William Roberts has written for many magazines and newspapers, including The Toronto Star *and* Harper's. *He is the author of* River in the Desert: Modern Travels in Ancient Egypt *and* In Search of the Birth of Jesus: The Real Journey of the Magi, *from which this story was excerpted.*

*

Maybe in order to understand mankind, we have to look at the word itself. Mankind. Basically, it's made up of two separate words—"mank" and "ind." What do these words mean? It's a mystery, and that's why so is mankind.

—Jack Handey, *Deeper Thoughts: All New, All Crispy*

Drawing by Chas. Addams; © 1974 The New Yorker Magazine, Inc.

DONNA MARAZZO

* ✳ *

Heeding the Call

The author drops her britches in Italy.

IF YOU'VE EVER SUCCESSFULLY PROGRAMMED A VCR, OR IF you are one of those people who actually know where "here" is on a map, then maybe, just maybe, you stand a chance in Italy's idea of a bathroom.

The sights of Italy will dazzle and amaze the most jaded traveler. The bathrooms of Italy will daze and confuse the most accomplished. Why? Because of the dizzying variety and configuration of toilets and their flushing mechanisms.

We arrived in Italy early in the morning and, after clearing customs (a mere wave of the hand and a formality stamp), boarded a bus for San Remo and the Italian Riviera. Enroute we stopped for refreshment at an Autogrill (actual real food served in a turnpike atmosphere—everything from freshly sliced cheeses and meats to wine on tap). Following our midmorning repast I felt the call of nature. I found my way to the Ladies, pushed open the door and stared. Facing me were ten eight-foot-high steel tubular contraptions. Had I detoured into the National Space

153

Center? Was I suppoed to enter one of these aluminum cans or wait until it blasted off?

I jump. A door suddenly slid open to reveal a woman, just as astounded as myself. She stepped out and smiled at me. One lamb to another? In I step. (Houston: we are Go.) The door slid closed. Okay, was I supposed to sit? Stand? Buckle up? A sign in several languages indicated the door would open automatically after five minutes. No dilly-dallying here, no catching up on the latest *Italian Vogue*. In fact, I was now so mortified that the door might slide open before my business and I had parted ways that I could no longer feel the urgent need to use the facility. (Houston: Abort; I repeat: Abort.)

Back on the bus I ruminated about my first encounter with the Italian version of bathroom crowd control. Okay, so now I knew what to expect. The next time. Right.

The bus circled down the mountainside into the coastal town of San Remo. As it did, it found every bump in the narrow strip of asphalt Italians refer to as roads. Each juggle, each bounce, each shimmy served to remind me of my failed earlier endeavor.

The hotel was a welcome sight. Our room looked out on the Mediterranean Sea. The terra cotta roofs, sprinkled like autumn leaves in the park, led down to the shore. I hesitated to enter the bathroom, expecting a steel coffin-like contraption. Instead, everything looked reasonably familiar. Almost American. Great, I recognized all the parts, except… hmmmm…where was…how did these things flush? After a frantic search I found a small pedal, pressed and whoosh. Away went, well, whatever, down the drain.

Yes, it seemed that Italy would present a totally unique travel challenge. By the end of our week in San Remo I thought I had mastered all Italy had to offer. But a fool and her confidence are soon parted.

A lunch in a side street *trattoria* turned into another bathroom adventure. One of our group went off to the Ladies and several minutes passed, then several more. After about fifteen minutes we began to worry. Was she sick? Lost? Was there a long line? My friends and I investigated. Tap, tap, tap on the lavatory door. Was that a voice inside? I opened the door and we entered. Our friend had managed to lock herself into the stall and could not operate the lock to release herself. I looked at it, my friends took a gander, I looked again. We might have been in Italy but the lock was Greek to us. Last resort—someone went to get help. Luckily, one of our group spoke Italian and was able to convey the seriousness of the situation to the *trattoria* manager. It didn't prevent him from doubling over in laughter. He did stop laughing long enough to explain in great detail, with much hand movement, my friend's situation to all who would listen. A line formed outside the bathroom as people crowded around to help extricate my friend from her small prison. A few tools later, liberation! Out she walked, red-faced and thoroughly embarrassed to the applause of everyone at the bar. Of course, after that ordeal a bottle of wine was in order and provided compliments of the house.

> From the moment I land on foreign soil until I return, my life is controlled by an author I've never heard of, who for all I know considers a hot shower to be as superfluous as a silver toothpaste key.
> —Margo Kaufman,
> *1-800 Am I Nuts?*

Week Two in Italy filled us with the hubris of the powder room proficient—we ventured forth as proud peacocks into the bathrooms of many an establishment, convinced, now, that we had faced all that Italy had to offer. But, like Pompeii in the early years of the first millennium, we also met our match at the foot of Mt. Vesuvius. In keeping with antiquity we found ourselves confronted by two grooves molded in the shape of foot prints and a dark hole in the dirt floor. In other words: the toilet.

The words "it's tough being a woman" take on a whole new meaning. Slip your feet into these puppies and tell me what you do with your jeans, your handbag, and your unmentionables. If you were fortunate enough ever to have played catcher on the company softball team you were at a definite advantage. With jeans tied in a bow around my neck and feet ensconced in their appointed spots (I felt ready to perform some ritualistic dance), a warm breeze cooling places best left untouched, I tried to enter a philosophical state and repeated my new mantra: "I will never complain about airline lavatories again, I will never complain...."

Donna Marazzo is a marketer with a major corporation by day and a writer by night who travels extensively for both business and pleasure. She has written two novels and is at work on a third, titled Racing Time, *which has nothing to do with heeding any of nature's calls. She lives in Philadelphia.*

＊

Early next morning, in the dark, I crept out behind our hut to the yucca plantation for a shit; flicking on my torch, I did my usual cursory erogenous zone-check—and then I looked again. In the cold dawn, the secret nightmare had finally clasped me: the Great Fear had come to stay. My penis had turned green. To the touch it felt like a hanging cluster of grapes. Swollen tapir ticks, as big as the top of a thumb, were feeding all down its stem. "Keep calm," I repeated out loud; and then I scrabbled at them, pulling them out, dropping them on the ground, popping them under my boot, yelping with pain....

Yes, said Chimo, laughing over a breakfast of meat and manioc, everybody knew, tapir ticks always climbed up a man's trousers and squeezed in sideways between his belt and his stomach—they went where every woman that he, Chimo, had ever known, in sixty years of service, always wanted to get her fingers.

—Redmond O'Hanlon, *In Trouble Again: A Journey
Between the Orinoco and the Amazon*

RALPH SCHOENSTEIN

* ✱ *

A New Tourist
in Town

*Even your back yard can feel foreign
with the right tour guide.*

BECAUSE THE MANHATTAN WHERE I GREW UP IS NOW situated near Oz, I was moved one early fall morning to inspect the replacement city with some tourists, to whom the Astor and the Roxy might have sounded like flowering plants. At the Gray Line terminal at Eighth Avenue and 54th Street, I paid $17 and climbed into the double-decker time warp, the kind of bus that had sent me airborne through the golden New York of just after World War II.

I was heady with the memory of travel on such open upper decks as the bus started north on Eighth Avenue and a young woman with an Eastern European accent began to talk through a mike.

"That is Al Pacino's apartment house," she said, pointing west at 56th Street, "and that building on other corner is where worked William Randolph Hearst, who was in movie *Citizen Kane.*"

"Was Al Pacino in that?" said a man in a Snoopy sweatshirt.

"No, just in building," she said. "And up there, on right,

is 160 Central Park South, where have apartments Pavarotti and Domingo."

A blast of jackhammers blocked her next historical insight, but as we turned up Broadway, I heard, "...and up there, on left, is Lincoln Center, built in 1960 by Mayor LaGuardia."

And a remarkable achievement indeed for a man who had died in 1947. Thinking fondly of LaGuardia, I gazed at massive gray piles of apartments west of Lincoln Center and wondered what he would have thought of buildings that blended the warmth of Stonehenge with the charm of East Berlin.

As our bus neared 72nd Street, the guide described the Art Deco style of the old Astoria apartment house, which had been an elegant right field wall for many of my stickball games. I felt a pang remembering two-sewer drives against a landmark.

"Darryl Hannah lives in that house," the guide went on to say, still seeing the city as a map in *People Magazine.* "And on far corner of next street, that is Dakota, first apartment house in New York. Built hundred years ago, where lived Lauren Bacall and Diana Ross and where John Lennon was shot. In Central Park is Strawberry Fields to memorize him."

When we turned up Central Park West and reached the American Museum of Natural History, where no celebrities lived, jackhammers assaulted us again, counterpoint to the constant sound of buses, cars, and trucks. "The roaring traffic's boom" was poetic in *Night and Day,* but the din of the nineties was deafening to someone trying to remember the soft postwar air. Unfortunately I still was able to hear the guide, who now began to tell us about the American Museum of Natural History. "Robert Redford shot movie there," she said.

She did, however, say that Central Park was a timeless

gem and that it was "where Jackie Kennedy rode her horse."

Passing the park at 94th Street, she told us about Columbia, my alma mater, which was only two miles away.

"Is oldest university in country," she said, but she didn't say which country. In this one, the oldest is Harvard. Nevertheless, her blend of fact and fancy seemed fitting for this fantastical city, where once I had seen a car being towed from a street called Liz Claiborne Avenue. What a fashionable place for a car to disappear.

A few minutes later, at 112th Street and Amsterdam Avenue, we stopped to visit the Episcopal Cathedral of St. John the Divine. Suddenly, it was 1943: the cathedral had been unfinished then and I could see no progress in 50 years, a nice change of pace for a city that sometimes defaces its architectural glories. New York turned the masterpiece that was Pennsylvania Station into an indoor street fair and smudged the wondrous twilight view south on Park Avenue by jamming in a building that belonged in Brasilia.

On the cathedral's main steps, workers from St. Luke's Hospital were eating heroes. Once again, I asked myself: "What does it all mean?" It meant they were not Episcopalians.

"Where are you from?" said a blond young man on the tour, who fell in step with me.

"I grew up in Manhattan," I said, "but I live in New Jersey now."

"Couldn't take the crime?"

"Yes, my landlord was a criminal. My rent just got too high."

Looking up at the soaring splendor of the huge cathedral, he was moved to say, "Guess you got nothing like this in New Jersey."

"Our best is the Brendan Byrne Arena," I said, "but we did finish it. Where are you from?"

"Tulsa."

"You like New York?"

"Sure. 'Cats' is really something. You think I should see the Statue of Liberty too?"

"Well, I don't know. After 'Cats' it all might be downhill."

When the bus began moving north again, the guide pointed right and said, "and that is Columbia Law School, where graduated Caroline Kennedy."

The guide's tone fit the dreaminess I felt as I moved above this latest version of the city, wondering why the French had ever said something as dumb as "the more things change, the more they stay the same." Would a Frenchman please take me to Ebbets Field?

As we turned west on 120th Street, the guide gestured to a building where my youngest daughter lives and said, "That is Barnard College, for girls from richest families in America. Cost $20,000 a year."

Barnard costs $28,000 a year if your daughter is selfish enough to want meals and a bed; and at least one student there is from a family that is counting on a religious miracle for financial aid.

Turning to a more stable part of the American scene, the guide now said, "That monument is tomb of General Grant. Was hero in War of Independence."

She was wise to have given Grant a new war because he needed fresh appeal: as a draw, his tomb has been a Yankee Euro Disney; and the dearth of tourists has saddened me, for I used to rollerskate outside the tomb, wondering if Grant had ever said anything better than "Let Us Have Peace."...

When the Hudson gave way to Harlem, the guide talked of the Apollo Theater, the Hotel Theresa and the Harlem Renaissance; but I was seeing too many people for whom no renaissance would ever come. Crossing Harlem with happy photographers, I felt uneasy.

After turning south, we reached the upper end of Central Park and the guide said, "Mount Sinai Hospital on left is where Ali McGraw died in *Love Story*…. And over there in Central Park is Great Lawn, where Paul Simon had big concert."

Her narrative style was to have the sound lead the picture by more than a mile: the Great Lawn was 30 blocks away. As we moved toward it, grand old buildings stood on my left, the earth's greatest park lay on my right, and a breeze began to blow on my face, all of which gave me the Manhattan high I had felt long ago when I'd tried to use this ride for romance. "Those Palisades," I once told a young woman, "they're just like the white cliffs of Dover, if the white cliffs of Dover were gray."

"And there is Central Park Mall," said the guide moments later, "Is like shopping mall."

Had Kmart arisen at the bandstand? It would not have surprised me in this city, where the improbable is the norm. On my next such ride, I might be seeing a renovated Grant's Tomb, turned into a historically correct condominium called the Appomattox Inn.

"Every room is a surrender to the past," Disney will say.

Ralph Schoenstein is a writer for The New York Times. *He wrote this piece for the Travel Section.*

*

The city bus tour: On one of these, you can sample the highlights of the city's traffic congestion, getting a terrific view of the entrances to some of Europe's most famous attractions. You will usually listen to a prerecorded history of these entrances on bus headphones that are precisely calibrated to always remain exactly ten minutes ahead of wherever your bus happens to be at the time. If you get bored, you can switch the channels and hear what static sounds like in other languages.

—Chris Harris, *Don't Go Europe*

* * *

Damp in the Afternoon

*Travel is the art of discovering how countries
that don't get* American Gladiators
entertain themselves.

WHEN I BEGAN TRYING TO DESCRIBE *TAUREAUX PISCINE* TO
people in America, I was struck by how many of them had
precisely the same response: "You have to be kidding!" I'll
admit that I might have been tempted to use that phrase myself when *taureaux piscine* first came to my attention, except
that my French wouldn't have been up to it. My French isn't
up to a lot, although I know a number of nouns. I probably
just shook my head in amazement, or did my imperfect imitation of that look Frenchmen in cafés use to indicate
without a word that what has just been said may well be
true for the simple reason that so many other silly things are.

    This happened one Saturday, market day, in Uzès. I was
sitting with Alice and Abigail and Sarah in an outdoor café
we favored on Saturdays for its proximity to our market-day
pommes frites specialist, a thorough craftsman who would not
consider offering a customer a sackful of French fries until he
had fried them at least twice. On a tree next to our table, a
handwritten sign announced an event that would take place

in the local arena at nine that night: TAUREAUX PISCINE. I do not have to be kidding.

I had been under the impression that both *taureaux* and *piscine* were among my nouns, but I couldn't think of any way to translate them except as "bulls" and "swimming pool." The next time our table was visited by the café's proprietress, a woman who had already demonstrated her good nature by a tolerant view of carried-in *pommes frites,* I tried to get some more information. *"Taureaux comme taureaux?"* I asked, using my fingers as horns to do a passable imitation of a fighting bull. (I know several conjunctions; it's verbs I don't do.)

"Oui, monsieur," she said.

"Piscine comme piscine?" I went on, demonstration with an

Esther Williams breaststroke that I happen to do almost flaw-
lessly as long as I'm out of the water.

"*Oui, monsieur.*"

She bustled off to see to her other customers, leaving me
with a lot of questions unexpressed and, for me in French,
unexpressible. I knew that the South of France, particularly
the area toward the mouth of the Rhône, had its own tradition of Provençal tauromachy. I suppose you could say that
the South of France, particularly the Côte d'Azur, has its own
tradition of swimming pools. But how would the two go
together? Why would the two go together?

The answers were not immediately forthcoming. As it
happened, we were unable to attend the *taureaux piscine* being
held in the arena that evening. We did have a couple of
English-speaking acquaintances who had lived in Uzès for
some time, but they had never heard of *taureaux piscine*. I
made a careful survey of wall posters in Uzès and in any other
town we happened to drive through that next week. No *taureaux piscine*. I began to think that I had missed the opportunity to see a unique coupling of bulls and swimming pool. It
occurred to me that I might be left with only that astound-
ing name—*taureaux piscine*. Aside from the energy it produced with its jarring juxtaposition, it had struck me from
the start as a name of great euphony. It was clearly at its best
when used as something like a war cry, with all four syllables
plainly and loudly enunciated—*"TAU-REAUX-PI-SCINE!"* In
fact, as we drove through the countryside around Uzès, I
occasionally found myself shouting *"TAU-REAUX-PI-SCINE"*
out the car window into the wind, as if to announce to the
residents of the next village what my quest was. The next
Saturday was our last Saturday in Uzès. We went to the same
café. I saw the same sign on the same tree: TAUREAUX PISCINE.

We arrived at the arena late. By chance, we had guests that weekend, and some of them were reluctant to rush through dinner, even though I kept telling them that, for all we knew about *taureaux piscine,* the best part might be right at the beginning. The arena looked like the bullfight arena of a Spanish provincial town except, of course, that in the middle of the ring there was a swimming pool—a rather small swimming pool, with only a couple of feet of water in it, but still a swimming pool. From the stands it looked like one of those plastic swimming pools that people in the suburbs buy at the discount store and stick out in the back yard for the smaller kids to splash around in. There were a few dozen teenage boys in the ring. There was also a bull—a small bull, with blunts on the points of his horns, but still a bull. In other words, the bull in *taureaux piscine* was a bull, and the swimming pool was a swimming pool. Upon my oath.

Within a few minutes it was clear that *taureaux piscine* has an extraordinary aspect that I had not anticipated during the week I'd spent simply amazed at its existence and enamored of its name. It is the only sport I have ever encountered that has only one rule: If you and the bull are in the pool at the same time, you win. If you do it again, you win again; a limitation of the rule would require a second rule.

The boys in the ring that night seemed to be having trouble winning. An announcer talked constantly over a public address system—exhorting the boys, taunting the boys, praising the bull, increasing the number of francs that would go to anybody who managed to share the pool with the bull. The boys, most of whom were dressed in blue jeans and t-shirts, spent a lot of time jumping up and down to attract the bull's attention and a lot of time running from the bull once they had it—usually ending the run by leaping over the inner fence that separates the ring from the stands in a bullfight arena. Occasionally, two or three of them would simply stand in the pool waiting for the bull to join them— like those towering but ungainly centers in the earlier days of basketball who planted themselves under the basket—and would have second thoughts about the strategy once the bull actually approached.

Suddenly, one boy, realizing that he had attracted the bull's attention from just the right angle, started his run toward the *piscine* simultaneously with the bull's charge and dived in head first just as the bull rumbled though the water. I thought it was a brilliant, daring move—something I might have been tempted to describe, if I had been a fan of longer duration, as "what *taureaux piscine* is all about."

Calvin Trillin is a staff writer for The New Yorker *and a columnist for* Time *and* The Nation. *He is also the author of several books including* Remembering Denny *and* Travels with Alice, *from which this was excerpted.*

*

To younger travelers: Don't embarrass us all by wearing a "Gamma Theta Phi 1st Annual Pole-Sitting and Raw Pig-a-Thon (Sponsored by Zeff's Auto Parts and WXLR 91 FM Golden Oldies Tower of Power Blast from Your Past Hot Hits), Bloomsburg State College, Greek Week Monster Blow-Out Bash 1992" plastered across your chest. Shirts like that confuse people in other countries. However, a discreet message affirming your concern for Gay Rainforest Whales would not be amiss and may even score points with a Young Euro.

—Thomas Neenan & Greg Hancock, *Let's Blow Thru Europe*

O.M. BODÈ

⁎ ⁎ ⁎

La Entrevista
(The Interview)

Outer space is closer than you think.

SOME YEARS AGO I HAPPENED TO BE IN THE HEADWATERS OF
the Amazon River at the port of Iquitos, Peru. I had just
flown across the Andes from Líma, having come from
Santiago de Chile, Easter Island and Tahiti. I was in a drifting
mood, living cheaply and seeing things that I had always
wanted to see.

Iquitos has been called the "Venice of Peru." Venice looks
nothing like Iquitos. You've seen pictures of Venice with historical buildings, canals with gondolas and the famous Piazza.
Well...Iquitos is a small South American city of churches,
nondescript white buildings turning yellow, dusty streets and
dilapidated wooden houses built on huge logs that float when
the river is high and sit in the mud when it is low. It is this
floating part of town that gives Iquitos it's nickname, "Venice
of Peru." Also it is known as "Belén," Spanish for Bethlehem.

It was dry season with low water when I was there. The
mud stank of sewage and bleach. Pigs and children investigated the brown muck. Next to this scene, a shrunken

Amazon River flowed by. Further downstream a few small river boats called "motos" were tied up at the bottom of a very high bank, which had some broken concrete steps strewn across its face, an attempt at one point by some city fathers to create a semblance of civilization on the edge of this anarchistic wilderness. Here the nicer aspects of civilization like the concrete steps get swept away, while the meaner ones stick like ticks on the back of a Zebu cow.

I stood in the heat at the top of the bank watching canoes and river boats in the act of dodging one another, logs, great masses of tree branches, river plants, motor oil cans, cardboard boxes and other flotsam.

A street urchin of about six or seven years old came up behind me and began playing with a collection of different-sized sticks. Glancing at her I could tell that she had great plans rumbling around in her small head. Her face would twist up in extreme concentration as she began to draw designs in the dirt. Then as she stepped back to study her opus her face would relax.

A jeep with an official emblem painted on it pulled up alongside of me. It had the Peruvian National Shield with the words *"Policías de Investigaciones Peruanas"* beneath it. Years later I read somewhere about the dreaded P.I.P…. Peep as it is known by its enemies.

A young man in full police uniform, dark glasses and classy brown boots stepped out and approached me. He was short and slender, because I remember him looking up at me. A holster with a huge automatic that looked like a Colt .45 graced his side. His pitch black hair was immaculately cut and he didn't have a mustache.

"Señor, de dónde eres?"

"Ah…Soy americano. Vengo de Líma."

"*Tiene usted pasaporte?*"

I pulled out my passport from my front pants pocket.

"*Yo no sé ingles. Sabe usted español, verdad?*"

"*Si señor, lo hablo.*"

"*Bíen. Qué haces aquí?*" (What are you doing here?)"

"Sight seeing."

"Where are you going?"

"Ah…I'm going to Brazil."

Alongside of us the little girl continued on her designs totally oblivious to this interrogation.

"Why did you specifically come to Iquitos?"

Each question was coming at me with machine gun rapidity.

"I want to find a river boat going down the Amazon to…ah, Tabatinga, Brazil."

He scrutinized my passport page by page, sometimes turning it around to read an elusive visa stamp. At last he came to the photograph of my face. Back and forth his eyes behind the dark glasses switched from the photo to my face. He was getting more suspicious by the minute, as if I wasn't the same person as my passport photo. Waves of paranoia swept across me. God, did I look that different! I was nervous and sweating profusely now.

Suddenly he stiffened even more and, slapping my passport on his thigh, asked, "What do you think of our government?"

"I…I don't know anything about your government."

Out of the corner of my eye I saw the little girl hike up her dirty dress and shoot a steady stream of urine on the ground in front of her. She was still oblivious to the *"extranjero"* and the *"polizonte"* standing beside her.

The police officer took no notice of her liquid act.

"Do you believe our government is corrupt?"

"Señor, I really haven't heard anything bad about your government. I've only been in Peru a week."

He handed my passport back to me.

"Well our government is crooked and corrupt. And," he waved his finger under my nose, "we are much poorer now than we were four years ago."

Now he was somewhat deflated from his earlier military posture. His shoulders were slightly bent forward, making him even shorter. He took off his dark glasses and looked at the river with angry eyes.

"I'm sorry to hear that." I volunteered, wondering whether this was some kind of trap to ensnare me, jail me and make me contact some rich parents or friends to pay my ransom. In reality, the very few friends I know who have money would probably be glad that I stayed in Peru. As for parents, my mother was dead and my father was living in the Canary Islands on a tiny pension. I would be doomed!

> I hope life isn't a big joke, because I don't get it.
> —Jack Handey, *Deeper Thoughts: All New, All Crispy*

He was silent and pensive for a few seconds.

A small river boat pulled away from the landing with hammocks swaying and chugged downstream towards Brazil on the thick reddish-brown water.

The street urchin was still with us. She had mixed up the urine and earth into a fine mud pie and was in the process of smoothing it out flat.

The policeman turned his gaze from the river and broke the silence with a sigh.

"Aahh…the other day I was driving on a road that goes

back into the jungle." Facing me he pointed vaguely down the river. "And…there was a small clearing that hadn't been there before and in it I saw a strange object. It was a…*platillo volador!*"

Sometimes when a person is speaking to you, you don't want him to think that you're not giving him your undivided attention by asking, "Huh?"

So I stayed silent as if I was seriously digesting what he had just said, when in reality I didn't know what the hell he was talking about. Meanwhile, with a small stick the child had begun to draw complex designs on the mudpie.

"Platillo volador." Of course, flying saucer! Images of Mexico City's taxis flitted across my mind. There was a custom there to have animal nicknames for different colored cabs like Cocodrilo, Mono and Papagayo. Maybe here in Peru they have nicknames for buses or funny looking old American automobiles.

"Un nave de espacio? (A space ship?)" I asked.

"Sí, sí un nave espacial con tripulación que salieron de una puerta en el casco, cuando se llegaba mi caro! (Yes, yes, a spaceship with crew members who exited from a door in the hull, when my jeep approached!)"

"Un nave de espacio?!" I mumbled incredulously.

"Sí. They were dressed in elegant uniforms made of some darkish green cloth with some kind of metal discs that covered only their right side which were too shiny to look at."

I looked at his eyes, which were focused somewhere in the distance above the trees on the horizon. It was as if he was re-living his adventures.

"They were very beautiful people, who looked like Earthlings, but were three meters tall and had white skin as white as the Paloma Blanca."

"Nave de espacio?!" I said for the third time, not sure whether I was hearing what I was hearing from this pillar of the establishment.

By now he was totally wrapped up in his own world, or maybe I should say, out of this one!

"They invited me on board and within fifteen seconds we had landed on Ganymede! Of course you know where Ganymede is? It is one of Jupiter's moons!"

Standing behind him the little artist was not satisfied with her mud pie moon. With an impatient look on her face she proceeded to cut the moon in half with a long stick.

"They had beautiful homes that were made out of intricate ice crystals. And surprisingly it wasn't cold!" He shook his head vigorously. "As I walked the ice pebbles beneath my feet played beautiful tunes and the music resounded and reflected through the houses. It was extraordinary!"

A small Indian woman in a dirty missionary dress passed us carrying some wooden poles strung with sun-dried piranhas. The vicious teeth flashed in the bright light. She stared at us suspiciously.

In the heat of the sun directly overhead my mind was trying to make some sense of this strange conversation. Space ships up the Amazon! Shades of *Chariots of the Gods.*

The kid had drawn and quartered her mud moon and was now in the process of stabbing each quarter with a smaller stick.

The erstwhile space traveler began gesticulating with his hands. "It seemed that I had only been there a few minutes, when my tall friends who spoke perfect Spanish, which sounded like children talking in a tunnel, told me that it was time to go back to Earth. It was very dangerous for me to stay there because many things were poisonous including their food. I was so excited I had forgotten how hungry I was, for I had only had a cup of coffee that morning."

By now I had decided to open up to him and get into whatever he was into. "*Muy interesante*, were you able to see Jupiter from Ganymede?"

He eyed me suspiciously and snapped,

"No, it wasn't visible. It was on the other side of Ganymede!"

"Oh."

"María…Maríangela. *Vente a casa*," called a distant voice. The mud pie artist perked up her ears.

"Maríiiaa, Maríiiiii…Angelaaaaa." Across the rooftops the call rose and fell along with the heat waves.

With a swift kick to one of the mud pie quarters, she took off, skipping down the dusty street, dragging her long stick across the doors and walls, making a rat-tat-bap-bang-whap-bap-tat-tat sound. One bap was across the face of a sleeping drunk lying against a wall. She disappeared around a corner.

"Again it only took fifteen seconds to traverse the distance between Ganymede and Earth. They left me by my jeep and departed. I sat there a few minutes, my head spinning, trying to understand what had happened to me."

When he said "spinning," a vision of him chewing nonchalantly on a piece of jungle mushroom or wiping his lips with some poisonous frog sweat, of course quite by accident, came to my mind.

He held his hands out, palms up, almost apologetically. I began to like this person. Anybody who has been to Ganymede can't be all bad.

"*Señor, por favor*, write down your address and when I get to New York, I'll send you some books about unidentified flying objects written in Spanish."

I looked at the small piece of brown paper getting wet with the sweat of my palm, then looked up at the fast disappearing jeep leaving a brown dust cloud down the road. *Muy interesante!*

O.M. Bodè *is a writer, photographer, and film editor who has been around the world ten times as a Merchant Seaman. His current home base is Hawaii.*

★

"You mind not smoking?"

It was the girl with the bags and the stony gaze.

I looked for a no smoking sign. There was none. I said, "Is it bothering you?"

She said, "It kills my eyes."

I put my pipe down and took a swig of beer.

She said, "That stuff is poison."

Instead of looking at her I looked into her bag. I said, "They say peanuts cause cancer."

She grinned vengefully at me and said, "Pumpkin seeds."

—Paul Theroux, *The Old Patagonian Express: By Train Through the Americas*

"*The map ends here, too!*"

DOUG LANSKY

* ✳ *

The Art of Riding a Third World Bus

Sometimes getting there is half the fun.
But usually it's not.

I HAVE AN IDEA FOR A NEW RIDE AT EPCOT CENTER, Disney's international theme park. It would be called: "The Developing Nation Bus Ride." I'm sure it would be a huge success because the last time I checked, every single ride at Disney had a four-hour line in front of it.

I'm often asked what I'm most afraid of when I travel to Third World countries. People expect to hear something like: catching the Ebola virus, being detained by the secret police, getting mugged in a dark alley, or catching the Ebola virus from the secret police in a dark alley. Now, I don't want to marginalize the image of any of these dramatic foreign tribulations, but they generally don't worry me. I mean, as tribulations go, they're right there at the top of the list. But riding a Third World bus has got to be one the most dangerous (and thrilling) rides on earth.

Here's how the The Developing Nation Bus Ride would work: Disney normally issues a single ticket for all attractions, but it wouldn't be valid for this ride. Part of the fun would be locating the place to buy the tickets, which would be secretly tucked away on the other side of the park. Tickets would be priced according to how much money the ticket vendor thought you were carrying, which would be determined by the estimated value of your jewelry, your clothes, and your camera.

Disney likes to entertain you while you wait for the ride to begin, and The Developing Nation Bus Ride would be no exception. Everyone would wait in a massive, filthy parking lot filled with buses. There would be several lines to stand in, but only one would actually get you to the right bus. While trying to figure out which line to choose, Disney taxi drivers would plead with you to ride with them for a "special price" and Disney pickpockets would try to relieve you of your valuables.

Upon reaching The Developing Nation Bus, any large items you were carrying would be taken from you and put on the roof, to be lost at a later time.

Then, you'd board the bus, which would be created by Disney's "imagin-eers" to look as though it were 50 years old, stolen from a junior high school in Oklahoma, and driven overland to, say, Bangladesh. The exterior would be painted with nine different, non-complementary colors and spattered with mud. The interior would be plastered with small Jesus figurines. The seats would be carefully designed to hold people the size of embryos and everyone would sit three-to-a-seat. Naturally, there would not be enough leg room for a chipmunk.

Mounted on a track, the bus would start to move, all the while simulating the effect of riding over huge craters in the road. There would be shock absorbers. But they would be crafted not to work.

Special vents in the bus would pipe in a lethal combination of second-hand smoke, dust, and sub-tropical body odor. As you began to cough, you'd wake up a realistic baby, who would cry uncontrollably in Dolby surround sound.

Then the afternoon sun, simulated by strong ultra-violet lamps, would overheat all the people on one side of the bus. To be fair, the other side would be treated to an intentionally dysfunctional heating system.

Professionally trained chickens would run up and down the aisle while Disney developing-nation families would continuously load and unload their worldly possessions from the small compartment located over your head. Sometimes the babies of the Disney families would puke a foul-smelling, but safe, green chunky substance all over you.

The bus would start to take wild turns as the bus driver would pretend to fall asleep. Then, just before he veered off the road and over a "cliff," he'd "wake up" and steer the bus back on course. However, he would immediately initiate a conversation with the people behind him while simultaneously watching the Bruce Lee movie playing on the TV mounted on the ceiling, just over his head.

> ———)———
>
> I bet a funny thing about driving a car off a cliff is, while you're in midair, you still hit those brakes! Hey, better try the emergency brake!
>
> ◆
>
> —Jack Handey, *Deeper Thoughts: All New, All Crispy*

You would drive past many beautiful vistas, but you wouldn't be able to see them because the windows would be smeared with a special high-tech chemical that simulates dirt.

Then the ride would stop momentarily so everyone could

get out and go to the toilet. Men would go to the bushes on one side of the road and women would go to bushes on the other. During the toilet break, an entire brigade of well-trained "locals" would descend on you and try to sell you very affordable little snacks that would, by the end of the ride, give everyone Disney dysentery.

Back on the bus you would find that someone had pretended to steal everything you'd left on board. There would be a large argument that would delay the bus ride for 30 minutes, but no one would be able to discover who took the missing items. A Disney policeman would arrive on the scene and write stolen-goods reports for people who were willing to bribe him.

Then you would drive across a pretend border into another country and everyone would have to get out and go through customs. A rigid Disney customs officer would fire a series of inane questions at you and then pretend to take 20 minutes to enter your name and passport number onto a carbon copy form (in quadruplicate) with his re-created 1930 Underwood typewriter that had half the keys pulled out.

While paying the customs official an extra $20 to speed up your visa application, you would no doubt begin to wonder why you picked The Developing Nation Bus Ride over the slighly calmer It's a Small World After All Ride, Tea Cup Ride, or the Dental Surgery Ride. Then you'd realize, it's a learning experience, a real adventure, and incredibly authentic!

Once back on board, the bus would drive around, apparently lost, for a few hours. Just as your lungs would be about to collapse from the simulated smoke, just as your eardrums would be about to burst from the simulated crying, and just as your spine would be about to pop a disk from the fake bouncing—The Developing Nation Bus Ride would come to an abrupt halt and Mickey Mouse would appear and lead you safely to the nearest exit.

Doug Lansky is the editor of this book, and the author of "Vagabond," a syndicated travel column that appears in newspapers throughout the United States.

＊

It's important to understand that in the Third World most driving is done with the horn, or "Egyptian Brake Pedal," as it is known. There is a precise and complicated etiquette of horn use. Honk your horn only under the following circumstances:

1. When anything blocks the road.
2. When anything doesn't.
3. When anything might.
4. At red lights.
5. At green lights.
6. At all other times.

—P. J. O'Rourke, *Holidays in Hell*

* ✳ *

The Wrong Number

*The author manages to find the language
barrier in a country that doesn't
really have one.*

I WENT TO THE STATION TO PURCHASE A TICKET ON THE NEXT morning's express to Stockholm. You cannot just hop onto a train in Sweden, but must think about it carefully and purchase a ticket in advance. The ticket hall had one of those systems where you take a number from a machine by the door and wait for it to appear above one of the ticket windows. My number was 415, and the highest number seeing action was 391. I waited for twenty minutes and the numbers advanced to 393, so I wandered off to the station news agent to look at girlie magazines. The news agent, alas, was closed, so I looked at a couple of travel posters, and then wandered back. Not entirely to my surprise, I discovered that there had been a frenzy of activity in my absence, and number 415 had come and gone. So I took another number—432 this time—and a seat and waited for half an hour. When at last my number came I presented myself at the window and asked the man for a ticket on the 10:05 to Stockholm the next morning.

He regarded me sadly, "I'm sorry, I do not speak English," he said.

I was taken aback. "Everybody in Sweden speaks English," I protested feebly.

His sadness grew. "I don't. Please you must to go to window sree." He indicated a window further down the line. "She speaks vair good English."

I went to window three and asked for a ticket to Stockholm the next morning. The woman, seeing the number 432 crumpled in my fist, pointed to the number above her window. "You have the wrong number. This window is for number 436." Even as she spoke a ferocious-looking lady with grey hair and a dicky hip was hoisting herself out of her chair and charging towards me. I tried to explain my problem with the monoglot at window five, but the ticket lady just shook her head and said, "You must take another ticket. Then maybe I will call you. Now I must deal with this lady."

"You are at zer wrong window!" the old lady announced in the bellow of someone whose hearing is going. "This is *my* window," she added, and tossed a haughty look to the rest of the room as if to say, Are foreigners stupid as shit, or what?

Forlornly I shuffled over to the machine and took another number. In fact, I took three—I figured this would give me some insurance—then retired to a new seat to watch the board. What a lot of fun I was having! Eventually my number came around again. It directed me to return to window number five—home of the only man in Sweden who speaks no English. I crumpled this ticket and waited for the next to be called. But he called the next one, too. I scampered to his window and begged him not to call my remaining number, but he did.

I couldn't bear to start the whole thing all over again.

"Please," I said, speaking carefully, "I just want a one-way ticket to Stockholm for tomorrow morning at 10:05."

"Certainly," he said, as if he had never seen me before, took my money and gave me a ticket. It's no wonder so many Swedes kill themselves.

Bill Bryson also contributed "Bill's Stroll Through Paris" to this book.

*

The first kind of strange toilet the traveler needs to get used to is the squatter, which looks like Chief from *One Flew Over the Cuckoo's Nest*, just picked up the john, threw it out the window, and ran from the crime scene, leaving a six-inch diameter hole in the floor right where the toilet is supposed to be. The idea is that you are supposed to squat over the hole and, like a B-2 Bomber, hit the target. Managing this requires a number of skills, none of which fell within the scope of my liberal arts degree which, for lack of toilet paper, would have really come in handy.

　　　　　　　　　—Doug Lansky, "Toilets Around the World"

Index of Contributors

Acknowledgements

I'd like to kiss on the lips all the people who made this book possible, starting with my girlfriend, Signe Mattsson, and then ending right after that. But I'd certainly be willing to give a warm embrace to my happily-divorced parents, Bruce and Vicki. And I'd like to hug or shake the hands of my fearless group of test readers and article spotters: Aaron Dorfman, Jens Andersson, Larry Bleiberg, Liz Bleiberg, Janet Fullwood, Carol Monaghan, Don George, Dana Lansky, Sean O'Reilly, Susan Brady, Jennifer Leo, Raj Khadka, Cindy Collins, Leili Eghbal, and Tim O'Reilly. Plus Dave Barry, for his blurb.

Last, but not least, and certainly deserving of this entirely separate paragraph, I'd like to thank James and Larry for being...well, the publishers. They were the ones who really...well, published the book. Which meant that they were probably responsible for several things...I guess. Actually, James and Larry played a very active role in all aspects of this book. They were tremendously encouraging; they carried the ball while I was on the road; and they were—especially when I managed to figure out the time-zone difference and call them at a reasonable hour—a delight to work with.

"Nudity is a State of Mind" by Alan Zweibel originally title "The Naked and the Red" and appeared in the July 1996 issue of *Los Angeles Magazine*. Reprinted by permission of the author. Copyright © 1996 by Alan Zweibel.

"Failing to Learn Japanese in Only Five Minutes" by Dave Barry reprinted from *Dave Barry Does Japan* by Dave Barry. Copyright © 1992 by Dave Barry. Reprinted by permission of Random House, Inc.

"Jugo Especial" by Lara Naaman published with permission from the author. Copyright © 1998 by Lara Naaman.

"Under the Spell of a Witch Doctor" by Rory Nugent excerpted from *Drums Along the Congo: On the Trail of Mokele-Mbembe, The Living Dinosaur* by Rory Nugent. Copyright © 1993 by Rory Nugent. Reprinted by permission of Houghton Mifflin Company. All rights reserved.

"An Irishman in Vurjinny" by Joseph O'Connor exerpted from *Sweet Liberty: Travels in Irish America* by Joseph O'Connor. Copyright © 1996. Reprinted by permission of Roberts Rinehart Publishers and Macmillan Publishers (UK).

"The Deep Fried Potato Bug" by Richard Sterling published with permission from the author. Copyright © 1998 by Richard Sterling.

"Down Jerky Road" by Sophia Dembling published with permission from the author. Copyright © 1998 by Sophia Dembling.

"Bill's Stroll Through Paris" and "The Wrong Number" by Bill Bryson extracted from *Neither Here Nor There: Travels In Europe* by Bill Bryson, published by Black Swan, a division of Transworld Publishers Ltd. Copyright © 1991 by Bill Bryson. Reprinted by permission of William Morrow Co. and Transworld Publishers, Ltd. All rights reserved.

"Dragging the Family to the Magic Kingdom" by Caryl Rivers originally appeared in the 1996 issue of *Grand Tour.* Copyright © 1996 by Caryl Rivers. Reprinted by permission of the author.

"A Simian in the Cinema" by Nigel Barley reprinted by permission of Harold Ober Associates Incorporated. Copyright © 1986 by Nigel Barley. From *Ceremony: An Anthropologist's Misadventures in the African Bush* (UK edition: *A Plague of Caterpillars*).

"Blinded by the White" by Mary Roach originally appeared in *Salon* magazine. Published by permission of *Salon* magazine and the author. Copyright © 1998 by Mary Roach.

"Shipping Out" by David Foster Wallace excerpted from *A Supposedly Fun Thing I'll Never Do Again* by David Foster Wallace. Copyright © 1997 by David Foster Wallace. Reprinted by permission of Little, Brown and Company, Inc.

"The Great Goat Race" by Peter Mayle excerpted from *A Year in Provence* by Peter Mayle. Copyright © 1989 by Peter Mayle. Reprinted by permission of Alfred A. Knopf, Inc. and Penguin Books Ltd.

"Out of Teheran" by John Krich excerpted from *Music in Every Room: Around the World in a Bad Mood* by John Krich. Reprinted by permission of the author. Copyright © 1984 by John Krich.

"A Holy Holiday in Hell" by P. J. O'Rourke excerpted from *Holidays in Hell* by P.J. O'Rourke. Copyright © 1988 by P.J. O'Rourke. Reprinted by permission of Grove/Atlantic.

"The Duck of Peace" by Carl Franz excerpted from *The People's Guide to Mexico* by Carl Franz, published by John Muir Publications, Santa Fe, NM 87504. Copyright © 1992 by Carl Franz.

"It's Monday...So This Must Be My Tax Write-Off in London" by Dave Barry excerpted from *Dave Barry Talks Back* by Dave Barry. Copyright © 1991 by Dave Barry. Reprinted by permission of Crown Publishers, Inc.

"Of Generals and Gentlemen" by David Arizmendi published with permission from the author. Copyright © 1998 by David Arizmendi.

"The Great Invisible Pheasant Hunt" by Jon Carroll reprinted from the September 11, 1996 issue of the *San Francisco Chronicle.* Copyright © 1996 by the *San Francisco Chronicle.* Reprinted with permission.

"Cena" by David Leavitt excerpted from from *Italian Pleasures* by David Leavitt

Additional Credits (arranged alphabetically by title)

Books, a division of Random House. Copyright © 1994 by Fran Lebowitz.

Selections from *Holidays in Hell* by P. J. O'Rourke copyright © 1988 by P. J. O'Rourke. Reprinted by permission of Grove/Atlantic.

Selections from *In Search of the Birth of Jesus* by Paul William Roberts reprinted by permission of The Putnum Publishing Group. Copyright © 1995 by Paul William Roberts.

Selection from *In Trouble Again: A Journey Between the Orinoco and the Amazon* by Redmond O'Hanlon copyright © 1988 by Redmond O'Hanlon. Reprinted by permission of Grove/Atlantic and Peters, Fraser & Dunlop Ltd.

Selection from "Keep 'Em Flying!" by Robert J. Matthews published with permission from the author. Copyright © 1998 by Robert J. Matthews.

Selection from Garrison Keillor reprinted by permission of the author. Copyright © 1998 by Garrison Keillor.

Selection from *Let's Blow Thru Europe* by Thomas Neenan and Greg Hancock reprinted by permission of Mustang Publishing Co., Inc. Copyright © 1989, 1992 by Thomas Neenan and Greg Hancock.

Selection from David Letterman reprinted by permission of Worldwide Pants, Inc.

Selection from George Lopez excerpted from *That's Funny* published by Andrews & McMeel and packaged by Cader Books.

Selection from Steve Martin reprinted by permission of the author and Michael Gendler.

Selections from *Neither Here Nor There: Travels In Europe* by Bill Bryson copyright © 1992 by Bill Bryson. Reprinted by permission of William Morrow Co. and Transworld Publishers, Ltd.

Selection from *The Obsessive Traveller, or, Why I Don't Steal Towels from Great Hotels Any More* by David Dale reprinted by permission of HarperCollins Publishers Pty Limited. Copyright © 1991 by David Dale.

Selection from *The Old Patagonian Express: By Train Through the Americas* by Paul Theroux copyright © 1979 by Cape Cod Scrivners Co. Reprinted by permission of Houghton Mifflin Company. All rights reserved.

Selections from *The Rants* by Dennis Miller reprinted by permission of Doubleday, a division of Bantam Doubleday Dell Publishing Group, Inc. Copyright © 1996 by Dennis Miller.

Selections from *The Size of the World: Once Around Without Leaving the Ground* by Jeff Greenwald reprinted with permission from the author. Copyright © 1995 by Jeff Greenwald. Originally published by The Globe Pequot Press.

Selections from "To Err is Humorous" by Sophia Dembling reprinted from the April 4, 1993 issue of *The Dallas Morning News*. Reprinted by permission of *The Dallas Morning News*. Copyright © 1993.

Selection from "Toilets Around the World" by Doug Lansky published with permission from the author. Copyright © 1998 by Doug Lansky.

Selection from "Travel Facts" by Sophia Dembling published with permission from the author. Copyright © 1998 by Sophia Dembling.

Selection from "Troglodytes in Gaul" by James O'Reilly reprinted from *Travelers' Tales France*. Reprinted with permission from the author. Copyright © 1995 by James O'Reilly.

Selection from *Unreliable Memoirs* by Clive James copyright © 1980 by Clive

James. Reprinted by permission of Alfred A. Knopf, Inc.

Selection from Henny Youngman excerpted from *That's Funny* published by Andrews & McMeel and packaged by Cader Books.

Cartoon Credits (arranged alphabetically by artist)

Drawing by Charles S. Addams reproduced by permission of The New Yorker Magazine, Inc. Copyright © 1974 by The New Yorker Magazine, Inc.

Drawing by Peter Arno reproduced by permission of The New Yorker Magazine, Inc. Copyright © 1938 by The New Yorker Magazine, Inc.

Drawing by Bruce Petty copyright © 1959 from The New Yorker Collection. Reprinted by permission. All rights reserved.

Drawings by Dan Piraro (Bizarro) copyright © by Dan Piraro. Reprinted with permission of Universal Press Syndicate. All rights reserved.

Drawing by James Stevenson copyright © 1975 from The New Yorker collection. Reprinted by permission. All rights reserved.

Drawings by Wiley copyright © 1993 by the Washington Post Writers Group. Reprinted by permission.

Drawings by Gahan Wilson originally appeared in *The New Yorker*. Reprinted by permission of the artist. Copyright © by GahanWilson.

About the Editor

Doug Lansky, a native Minnesotan, has been backpacking around the world since May 1992 when he graduated from Colorado College with a B.A. in a subject he can no longer recall. He has visited over 60 countries, chronicling his humorous adventures in his nationally-syndicated newspaper column, "Vagabond" and on National Public Radio's Savvy Traveler program. When Doug is not blowgun hunting with Jaguar Indians in Peru, test driving Ferraris in Italy, reindeer herding in the Arctic Circle, picking grapes in France, or sailing down the Nile on a Felucca, he tries to get a little rest in Sweden, his most recent base camp.

TRAVELERS' TALES GUIDES

LOOK FOR THESE TITLES IN THE SERIES

$\mathscr{S}$PECIAL INTEREST

THE GIFT OF TRAVEL:
The Best of Travelers' Tales
Edited by Larry Habegger, James O'Reilly & Sean O'Reilly
ISBN 1-885211-25-2, 240 pages, $14.95

THERE'S NO TOILET PAPER ON THE ROAD LESS TRAVELED:
The Best of Travel Humor and Misadventure
Edited by Doug Lansky
ISBN 1-885211-27-9, 207 pages, $12.95

A DOG'S WORLD:
True Stories of Man's Best Friend on the Road
Edited by Christine Hunsicker
ISBN 1-885211-23-6, 257 pages, $12.95

Check with your local bookstore for these titles
or call O'Reilly to order:
800-998-9938 (credit cards only—weekdays 6AM–5PM PST)
707-829-0515, or email: order@oreilly.com

$\mathcal{W}$OMEN'S TRAVEL

SAFETY AND SECURITY FOR WOMEN WHO TRAVEL
By Sheila Swan & Peter Laufer
ISBN 1-885211-29-5, 159 pages, $12.95

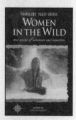

WOMEN IN THE WILD:
True Stories of Adventure and Connection
Edited by Lucy McCauley
ISBN 1-885211-21-X, 307 pages, $17.95

A MOTHER'S WORLD:
Journeys of the Heart
Edited by Marybeth Bond & Pamela Michael
ISBN 1-885211-26-0, 233 pages, $14.95

A WOMAN'S WORLD:
True Stories of Life on the Road
Edited by Marybeth Bond
Introduction by Dervla Murphy
ISBN 1-885211-06-6
475 pages, $17.95

———— ⋆ ✶ ⋆ ————

Winner of the Lowell Thomas Award for Best Travel Book—Society of American Travel Writers

GUTSY WOMEN:
Travel Tips and Wisdom for the Road
By Marybeth Bond
ISBN 1-885211-15-5, 123 pages, $7.95

*W*OMEN'S TRAVEL

GUTSY MAMAS:
Travel Tips and Wisdom for
Mothers on the Road
By Marybeth Bond
ISBN 1-885211-20-1, 139 pages, $7.95

*B*ODY & SOUL

THE ROAD WITHIN:
True Stories of Transformation
and the Soul
Edited by Sean O'Reilly, James O'Reilly
& Tim O'Reilly
ISBN 1-885211-19-8, 459 pages, $17.95

LOVE & ROMANCE:
True Stories of Passion on the Road
Edited by Judith Babcock Wylie
ISBN 1-885211-18-X, 319 pages, $17.95

FOOD:
A Taste of the Road
Edited by Richard Sterling
Introduction by Margo True
ISBN 1-885211-09-0
467 pages, $17.95

THE FEARLESS DINER:
Travel Tips and Wisdom for Eating
around the World
By Richard Sterling
ISBN 1-885211-22-8, 139 pages, $7.95

COUNTRY GUIDES

AMERICA
Edited by Fred Setterberg
ISBN 1-885211-28-7, 550 pages, $19.95

JAPAN
Edited by Donald W. George
& Amy Greimann Carlson
ISBN 1-885211-04-X, 437 pages, $17.95

INDIA
Edited by James O'Reilly & Larry Habegger
ISBN 1-885211-01-5, 538 pages, $17.95

ITALY
Edited by Anne Calcagno
Introduction by Jan Morris
ISBN 1-885211-16-3, 463 pages, $17.95

FRANCE
Edited by James O'Reilly, Larry Habegger
& Sean O'Reilly
ISBN 1-885211-02-3, 517 pages, $17.95

COUNTRY GUIDES

MEXICO

Edited by James O'Reilly & Larry Habegger
ISBN 1-885211-00-7, 463 pages, $17.95

THAILAND

Edited by James O'Reilly
& Larry Habegger
ISBN 1-885211-05-8
483 pages, $17.95

SPAIN

Edited by Lucy McCauley
ISBN 1-885211-07-4, 495 pages, $17.95

NEPAL

Edited by Rajendra S. Khadka
ISBN 1-885211-14-7, 423 pages, $17.95

BRAZIL

Edited by Annette Haddad & Scott Doggett
Introduction by Alex Shoumatoff
ISBN 1-885211-11-2
452 pages, $17.95

CITY GUIDES

HONG KONG
Edited by James O'Reilly, Larry Habegger & Sean O'Reilly
ISBN 1-885211-03-1, 439 pages, $17.95

PARIS
Edited by James O'Reilly, Larry Habegger & Sean O'Reilly
ISBN 1-885211-10-4, 417 pages, $17.95

SAN FRANCISCO
Edited by James O'Reilly, Larry Habegger & Sean O'Reilly
ISBN 1-885211-08-2, 491 pages, $17.95

SUBMIT YOUR OWN TRAVEL TALE

Do you have a tale of your own that you would like to submit to Travelers' Tales? We highly recommend that you first read one or more of our books to get a feel for the kind of story we're looking for. For submission guidelines and a list of titles in the works, send a SASE to:

Travelers' Tales Submission Guidelines
P.O. Box 610160, Redwood City, CA 94061

or send email to ***ttguidelines@online.oreilly.com***
or visit our Web site at **www.oreilly.com/ttales**

You can send your story to the address above or via email to ***ttsubmit@oreilly.com***. On the outside of the envelope, ***please indicate what country/topic your story is about***. If your story is selected for one of our titles, we will contact you about rights and payment.

We hope to hear from you. In the meantime, enjoy the stories!